THE DESIGN AND MANUFACTURE OF ANIMAL-DRAWN CARTS

Prepared for the International Labour Office (ILO)
and the United Nations Centre for Human Settlements (Habitat)

INTERMEDIATE TECHNOLOGY PUBLICATIONS 1986

Practical Action Publishing Ltd
27a Albert Street, Rugby, CV21
2SG, Warwickshire, UK
www.practicalactionpublishing.org

© Intermediate Technology Publications 1986.

First published 1986\Digitised 2013

ISBN 10: 0 94668 852 4
ISBN 13: 9780946688524
ISBN Library Ebook: 9781780441948
Book DOI: http://dx.doi.org/10.3362/9781780441948

All rights reserved. No part of this publication may be reprinted or reproduced or utilized in any form or by any electronic, mechanical, or other means, now known or hereafter invented, including photocopying and recording, or in any information storage or retrieval system, without the written permission of the publishers.

A catalogue record for this book is available from the British Library.

The authors, contributors and/or editors have asserted their rights under the Copyright Designs and Patents Act 1988 to be identified as authors of this work.

Since 1974, Practical Action Publishing (formerly Intermediate Technology Publications and ITDG Publishing) has published and disseminated books and information in support of international development work throughout the world. Practical Action Publishing is a trading name of Practical Action Publishing Ltd (Company Reg. No. 1159018), the wholly owned publishing company of Practical Action. Practical Action Publishing trades only in support of its parent charity objectives and any profits are covenanted back to Practical Action (Charity Reg. No. 247257, Group VAT Registration No. 880 9924 76).

CONTENTS

	Page
PREFACE	ix

1. INTRODUCTION
   Background — 1
   Scope and content — 3
   How to use the memorandum — 4

2. CHARACTERISTICS AND ASSESSMENT OF CARTS
   2.1 Introduction — 7
   2.2 Cart Configuration — 9
       2.2.1 Two-Wheeled Carts — 9
           Two-wheeled carts with solid-tyred wheels — 9
           Two-wheeled carts with pneumatic-tyred wheels — 10
           Tool carriers — 13
       2.2.2 Four-Wheeled Carts — 13
   2.3 Animal Draught — 14
       2.3.1 Animals — 14
           Types of animal — 14
           Performance of animals — 14
       2.3.2 Harnessing and Hitching Arrangements — 17
           Bovine harnesses — 17
           Equine harnesses — 18
           Camel harnesses — 18
           Hitching of a single animal — 18
           Hitching of more than one animal — 19
   2.4 Bodywork — 20
       2.4.1 General Purpose Bodywork — 20
       2.4.2 Special Purpose Bodywork — 21
           Passenger carrying — 21
           Ambulance — 22
           Water carrier — 22
           Water bowser — 22
           Tipping cart — 22
           Bottom-dumping cart — 22
           Stake-sided cart — 23
   2.5 Wheel/Axle Assembly — 23
       2.5.1 Wheel and Tyre — 23
           Wooden wheels — 23
           Spoked steel wheels — 24
           Solid tyres — 25
           Pneumatic-tyred wheels — 25
       2.5.2 Axle — 26
           Dead axle — 26
           Live axle — 27
           Motor vehicle axles — 27
           Axles for four-wheeled carts — 27
       2.5.3 Bearings — 28
           Plain bearings — 28
           Rolling element bearings — 28
       2.5.4 Suspension — 29
       2.5.5 Brakes — 29
   2.6 Selection Method — 30

			Page

3. GUIDELINES ON CART DESIGN
   3.1 General Design Considerations 33
      3.1.1 Functional Requirements 33
      3.1.2 Aesthetic Requirements 33
      3.1.3 Cost Considerations 34
      3.1.4 Manufacturing Considerations 34
   3.2 Technical Details - Cart Structure 35
      3.2.1 Major Dimensions 35
      3.2.2 Frame Construction 36
      3.2.3 Axles 38
      3.2.4 Suspension 39
      3.2.5 Harness and Hitching Arrangements 39
      3.2.6 Bodywork 41
   3.3 Technical Details - Wheel Assembly 42
      3.3.1 Wheels 42
      3.3.2 Tyres 45
      3.3.3 Bearings 46
         Plain bearings 46
         Rolling element bearings 47
      3.3.4 Brakes 48

4. MANUFACTURING ASPECTS
   4.1 Introduction 51
   4.2 Methods and Scale of Production 51
      4.2.1 Village Craftworkers 51
      4.2.2 Formal Sector De-Centralised Workshops 53
      4.2.3 Centralised Large-Scale Production 54
   4.3 Production Engineering 55
      4.3.1 Production Tooling 55
      4.3.2 Quality Control Procedures 57
   4.4 Production Organisation and Management 58
      4.4.1 Production Costs 58
         Direct labour cost 59
         Direct material cost 60
         Overheads 61
         Calculation of total unit production cost 63
      4.4.2 Selling Price 64

ANNEX: TRACTIVE EFFORT
   Gradient of the terrain 68
   Roughness and hardness of the route surface 68
   Total weight of the cart 68
   Position of the centre of gravity of the total weight 69
   Diameter of the wheels 69
   Width of the wheel rim 69
   Type of tyre 69
   Bearing friction 70
   Line of draught 70
   Acceleration of cart 70

REFERENCES 71

ILLUSTRATIONS

Figures 2.1 - 2.40 appear between pages 32 and 33

Figures 3.1 - 3.24 appear between pages 49 and 51

ACKNOWLEDGEMENTS

The Publishers would like to thank the following organizations and individuals for use of illustrations and other published material:

The Bureau of Highways, Ministry of Communication, China for Figs. 2.11 and 2.30; CAMARTEC, Arusha, Tanzania for Fig. 3.3; the Central Institute of Agricultural Engineering, Bhopal, India for Figs. 3.1 and 3.2; Dunlop India Ltd., Calcutta, India for Figs. 3.5 and 3.24; Economic and Social Commission for Asia and the Pacific, Bangkok, Thailand for Fig. 2.37; German Appropriate Technology Exchange (GATE), Eschborn, W. Germany for Figs. 2.5, 2.35, 3.6, 3.8, 3.12, 3.14, 3.15, 3.22, 3.23; Goe, M.R. and McDowell, R.E., Cornell University, New York for Table 2.3; Gowen, H.C., Al Khobar, Saudi Arabia for Fig. 2.12; the India Standards Institute for Table 3.1 and Fig. 3.21; Profile Books Ltd., Windsor, Berks, UK and the Worshipful Company of Wheelwrights, UK for Fig. A1.

PREFACE by the ILO and UNCHS/HABITAT

At present, the majority of people in developing countries are not adequately served by transportation systems. In rural areas, most people live at a considerable distance from a conventional road, and, in spite of great efforts to develop rural road networks, there is little hope that an optimal road density will be reached in the foreseeable future. Moreover, even in areas where settlements have access to roads, the economic conditions do not permit a large increase in the use of conventional motorised vehicles on an extended road network.

Few people in developing countries can afford either to own or use a conventional motor vehicle, yet traditional means of transport are ignored by those responsible for the planning and development of transport in developing countries. Therefore, human porterage is still the main way by which the poor move goods in many areas, and a great number of personal trips are made on foot. Generally, the inadequacies of existing transport systems are a constraint on economic and social development.

It is becoming increasingly apparent that the conventional approach to local transport development cannot respond to the transport needs of most of the low-income population. Among various measures which would change the present situation, an important one is the wide-scale promotion of efficient low-cost forms of transportation. There is a range of such transportation forms, both motorised and non-motorised, found in different countries, and considerable potential for the transfer of technologies. There are also possibilities for improving traditional designs.

It is with this in mind that the ILO and UNCHS/HABITAT have initiated the preparation of a series of technical memoranda on low-cost vehicles. The purpose of these studies is to provide a simple guide to the design and manufacture of these vehicles so that (a) the technology is made known to a wide audience, including decision-makers and planners who should be aware of the potential range of proven low-cost vehicles, and (b) producers are provided with information and guidelines on the design and manufacturing procedures which can be employed in various circumstances and at different scales of production. The first technical memorandum in the series relates to animal-drawn carts.

While animal-drawn carts have been used for hundreds of years in many countries, there have been few attempts to explain the principles of good design or to describe suitable manufacturing methods using contemporary materials and technologies. In a few countries, traditional cart-construction skills are still available, but in many others no such body of knowledge is to be found. This prevents the widespread use of abundant draught-animal power for transport.

Animal-drawn carts have considerable potential for widespread use because they are (a) capable of meeting local transport needs efficiently, (b) not restricted to use on motorable roads, (c) affordable and socially acceptable, (d) powered by renewable sources of energy, and (e) suitable for production and maintenance using mainly local resources. Generally, animal-drawn carts can play an important role in providing efficient and cheap transportation to move farm produce and inputs, water for domestic and productive use, building materials, commercial goods, solid waste, etc. Furthermore, local production of vehicles can offer opportunities for generating new employment openings in both the formal and informal sectors.

It is often suggested that efforts should be focused on promoting mechanised, rather than animal-based, means of transport. However, the widespread use of motorised vehicles is dependant on the users' ability to find the necessary financial resources and on the existence of motorable roads and technical support services. Moreover, in many countries, the costs of importing oil are a limiting factor. Thus, while a steady growth in mechanisation of transport is inevitable, animal-drawn transport can still play a significant role.

Future publications in this series will deal with low-cost mechanised vehicles and with pedal-driven vehicles.

This volume has been prepared for the ILO and UNCHS/HABITAT by Ian Barwell and Gordon Hathway of I.T. Transport Ltd. (United Kingdom).

CHAPTER 1: INTRODUCTION

Background

The past decade has seen increasing interest in the use of draught animal power for agriculture and, to a lesser extent, for transport. More and more developing countries are accepting that the use of animal power is a necessary stage in the process of transforming low output subsistence farmers, equipped with primitive hand tools, into high productivity mechanised producers. Also, draught animals provide a valuable source of power which use only renewable sources of energy. Although there are now many programmes aimed at the establishment of animal-based agricultural systems, the development of efficient forms of transport has tended to lag behind improved forms of cultivation and harvesting.

This is in some respects surprising since, as the FAO observed many years ago, the farmer is, above all else, a transporter. Efficient farming requires that inputs in the form of seeds, fertilisers, insecticides and pesticides are supplied in the right amounts at the right time. Equally, that farm produce is moved to market or store when optimum growth has been achieved. Even for subsistence level operations, the weight of such goods movement generated by one household can exceed several tonnes in a year, and there is evidence from many studies that these transport requirements are already a constraint on small farmer output. In seeking to improve agricultural output, it is therefore essential that the means of transport involved be improved accordingly.

Access to an animal-drawn vehicle can offer a simple, manageable and affordable improvement over existing methods of transport, which frequently consist simply of human portering. Ownership, or even the ability to hire the use, of a cart frees the farmer from dependence on motor vehicle services which are often unreliable and costly. Moreover, carts have a carrying capacity that is much more suitable for the majority of the farmers' relatively small-load, short-distance movement needs. They also have the ability to operate across fields and along paths and tracks that generally cannot be used by motor vehicles. The provision of roads and motor vehicles can solve only a part of the farmers' transportation needs, because these forms of transport are orientated toward movement between a goods collection point and central market, rather than between farm and collection point. It is only recently that recognition has been given to the magnitude of goods movement needs associated with on-farm and farm-to-collection point transport. In villages remote from the road system lack of efficient transport for these activities results in a very considerable loss of potential cash income for farmers. Existing methods are often arduous and time consuming, limit the ability to move produce, and consequently limit the incentive to produce more. The lack of efficient local transport can also lead to exploitation by the few traders who do reach the villages. If a farmer is able to move his produce to a collection point then he can expect a better return for his labour.

Two- and four-wheeled carts drawn by oxen, horses, donkeys, mules or camels are extensively used for farm transport in certain countries. They have considerable potential for more widespread use since they:

- are capable of meeting rural movement needs efficiently;

- are affordable and socially acceptable;

- can be produced and maintained using mainly local resources, thereby creating employment opportunities;

- are not restricted to use on motorable roads;

- can be made widely available because of their low capital cost.

There is another important consideration. Even if animals are used for all the major agricultural activities: land preparation, seeding, weeding and harvesting, the animals are only worked for relatively short periods of the year. If the same animals are also used for transport the cost of their upkeep can be spread over a greater amount of useful work. They may also enable the farmer to earn revenue through hire charges. Moreover, and especially where animal power is being introduced for the first time or the beasts are young, the regular use of animals for transport as well as agricultural operations maintains their familiarity with working in harness.

In countries where the use of animal carts is widespread it is not just farmers who benefit from their use. Many people earn a living in their construction and maintenance. Carts are also used by many artisans, service trades, construction and transport industries. They are particularly useful for short distance, suburban and urban-rural trips that would be relatively expensive by motor vehicle.

A well-designed cart greatly increases the load that can be moved by animals in comparison with that which can be carried on their back or pulled on a sledge. Carts should be light in weight yet strong, have efficient wheel/axle systems that are simple to manufacture and be equipped with an efficient means of harnessing the animals. Whilst none of these requirements is technically demanding, experience has shown that if such devices are to be produced and used successfully then they must be:

- adapted carefully to local operating conditions in terms of terrain, type of use and the characteristics of indigenous draught animals;

- designed to take account of local production conditions in terms of the availability of components, materials and manufacturing skills;

- manufactured in a way and on a scale that matches the capabilities of local industry;

● marketed at a price people can afford, with credit available if necessary.

Whilst animal carts have been used for hundreds of years in many countries there have been few recent attempts to explain the principles of good design, or to describe manufacturing methods suitable for current materials and technologies. In a few countries traditional cart construction skills are still freely available, but in many others no such body of knowledge is to be found. Consequently, the International Labour Organisation (ILO) and the United Nations Centre for Human Settlements (HABITAT) have joined efforts in order to improve the dissemination of information on appropriate animal cart technologies among developing countries.

Scope and content

This technical memorandum is concerned with the design and manufacture of _efficient_ animal-drawn carts. It provides detailed information on animal cart design and the manufacturing technologies that might be employed under different circumstances and at different scales of production. It forms one of a series of technical memoranda which are mostly intended for producers, and potential producers, who have some difficulties in choosing and applying technologies best suited to their own circumstances. However, they are also of interest to public planners, project evaluators from development agencies, training institutions and national and international financial institutions. In short, the memoranda should be useful to all those who are in a position to influence the choice of public or private investment and therefore the choice of technologies associated with these investments.

Chapter 2 provides a description and assessment of the characteristics of different types of animal-drawn cart. A comparative analysis is made of the advantages and disadvantages of different types of cart in terms of parameters such as:

- cost;
- load carrying capability;
- speed of travel;
- performance efficiency;
- terrain capability;
- use of local resources;
- ease of maintenance.

This analysis provides the information necessary to assess the performance potential of different types of cart, and to prepare an overall specification of the most appropriate type to suit a particular set of conditions of manufacture, ownership and operation.

Chapter 3 provides detailed technical guidelines on cart design, based on examples of several different types incorporating different features.

Chapter 4 discusses the organisation, management and production engineering aspects of manufacture, and considers the advantages, disadvantages and practical implications of manufacturing carts at different scales of production. The chapter describes various methods of improving production efficiency to increase productivity, reduce costs and achieve good product quality. Finally there is an analysis of manufacturing costs, and discussion of the considerations involved in setting sales prices.

The Annex discusses the subject of tractive effort, which is of central importance in determining a cart's performance and efficiency, and is affected by many design parameters.

The technical memorandum is not intended as a training manual. It is assumed that potential users of the technologies described in the memorandum are trained practitioners and the memorandum is only supposed to provide them with information on alternative technological choices. The memorandum may, however, be used as complementary training material.

How to use the memorandum

The approach adopted throughout is to present a range of options from which readers can select the most appropriate to suit their own circumstances. In Chapter 2, a range of different types of cart and cart features are described. In Chapter 3, various design options to suit different materials and manufacturing methods are presented. In Chapter 4, different methods of manufacture and scales of production are described.

Where animal-drawn carts are already in widespread use the main requirement is likely to be for improvement, rather than the introduction of wholly new designs. Chapter 2 will enable existing designs to be assessed, and the potential for improvement to be identified. The element by element descriptions in Chapter 3 offer scope for making improvements gradually, and for improved components to be fitted to existing carts.

Where few animal carts exist, the information in Chapters 2 and 3 is presented in such a way that new and appropriate designs can be developed methodically. Chapter 2 provides the basis for preparing the overall specification of a cart to suit particular circumstances. To assist in this a 'selection method' is included at the end of the chapter. This consists of a series of questions to be answered by the reader, with reference to the preceding information, with the aim of developing the specification step by step. The emphasis throughout is on consideration of the needs of the intended owner or user. Chapter 3 then provides the cart designer with the technical information necessary for the preparation of a detailed design within the framework provided by the overall specification. The chapter is structured to enable the design to be developed step by step.

Chapter 4 will provide additional information for the designer when considering manufacturing methods. It will also enable those involved in cart production to improve existing methods and calculate production costs accurately. The description of different types of manufacturing organisation and scales of production will be of most interest to planners concerned with the development of the manufacture and use of animal-drawn carts from a national perspective.

CHAPTER 2: CHARACTERISTICS AND ASSESSMENT OF CARTS

2.1 Introduction

The purpose of this chapter is to provide a description and assessment of the characteristics of different types of animal-drawn cart. The chapter makes a comparative analysis of the advantages and disadvantages of different types of cart in terms of parameters such as:

- cost;
- load carrying capability;
- speed of travel;
- performance efficiency;
- terrain capability;
- use of local resources;
- ease of maintenance.

This analysis provides the information necessary to assess the performance potential of different types of cart, and to prepare an overall specification of the most appropriate type to suit a particular set of conditions of manufacture, ownership and operation.

The specification of a particular type of cart can be broken down into four basic elements:

Cart Configuration — the number and type of wheels used, and the type of frame construction.

Animal Draught — the number and type of animals used to pull the cart, the type of harness used and the method of hitching the animal(s).

Bodywork — the type of bodywork fitted to the basic structure of the cart, and hence its usefulness for carrying different types of load.

Wheel/Axle Assembly — the type of wheels, tyres and bearings used, the method of mounting the wheels on the cart, and the use of suspension and brakes.

The specification of each of these elements is independent of the others to a significant degree. It is therefore most useful to assess the characteristics of carts element by element. Thus the approach adopted in this chapter is to analyse the advantages and disadvantages of different specifications for each element. This information can then be assembled to make an overall assessment of a particular design of cart using the 'selection method' presented at the end of the chapter. Similarly, the information can be analysed to prepare an appropriate cart specification to suit particular conditions.

This chapter concentrates on:

i) the types of cart which are in widespread use in developing countries and of which there is substantial operational experience available; and

ii) recent innovations and developments in cart design, which are relevant to developing country conditions, and which are now being applied, or could beneficially be applied, to improve the performance, usefulness or economic viability of animal-drawn carts.

However, it is also useful to understand something of the history of animal-drawn carts, not only in those developing countries where they are a traditional means of transport, but also in the industrialised world. In Europe and North America animal-drawn carts were the principal means of land transport until the motor vehicle became popular at the beginning of the 20th century. The performance of some of the horse-drawn vehicles was remarkable. In the early 19th century English mail coaches regularly made a 420km journey in 27 hours, averaging more than 20km/hr on certain sections (1). To achieve this required elaborate organisation and many changes of horses, a system of operation that is not relevant to developing country conditions, but the example does illustrate the performance potential of animal-drawn carts. Looking at another aspect of performance, four-wheeled wooden wagons drawn by two horses, with a carrying capacity of three to four tonnes, were used in great numbers to move agricultural goods (2).

The most extensive traditional and current use of animal-drawn carts in developing countries is in Asia, primarily in the Indian subcontinent and China. In present day India some 15 million animal carts are estimated to be in use, moving about 15,000 million tonne-km of goods per year. It has been estimated that about 80% of these carts are located in the rural areas, but that they are operated more intensively in urban areas, where trip distances tend to be longer, loads greater, and the animals are little used for other purposes (3). Most of these carts are of traditional two-wheeled wooden construction, made by local carpenters, and drawn by one or two bullocks, although a small proportion (about 5-10%) have pneumatic tyres and rolling element bearings. In Sri Lanka in 1978 there were twice as many bullock carts in use as there were lorries and tractor-trailers (4). Most of these were similar to the traditional Indian type. In China, which also has a long history of using animal carts, a conscious effort was made by the Government in the 1950's to increase the efficiency of traditional vehicles. Special factories were set up for the large-scale manufacture of steel axles and wheel rims, pneumatic tyres and ball bearings, which could be incorporated into otherwise traditional types of cart. A wide variety of different carts are now in use there, with capacities up to 8 tonnes, many of them benefiting from the improved technology (5).

2.2 Cart Configuration

The two basic configurations of animal-drawn cart are two-wheeled and four-wheeled. In assessing the characteristics of two-wheeled carts an important distinction is between those with solid-tyred wheels and those with pneumatic tyres. The distinction is not relevant to four-wheeled carts because it is highly unlikely that these would be constructed other than with pneumatic-tyred wheels nowadays. In this section reference is made to the payload capacity and weight of different configurations of cart. It is important to understand that payload capacity depends on other factors as well as the configuration of the cart, so that the figures given here should only be used as indications of likely capacity. Except for very specialised applications, carts will be made from wood (or bamboo), steel or a combination of the two. The strength and weight of the cart will depend upon the materials used, and the efficiency with which they are utilised in the construction of the cart. However detailed consideration of the use of materials is covered in chapter 3.

2.2.1 Two-Wheeled Carts

The most common type of animal cart has two wheels either side of a load platform, positioned so that the centre of the load area is close to the axle of the wheels. These carts are usually pulled by one animal or a pair of animals. Two-wheeled carts are relatively simple to make, cheap to purchase and easy to manoeuvre and control. A crucial characteristic of two-wheeled carts is that the draught animal(s) acts as the third point of support and carries part of the weight of the cart and its payload. There are many different types of two-wheeled cart but it is convenient to categorise them in terms of the wheel and tyre used.

Two-wheeled carts with solid tyred-wheels

Solid-tyred wheels were the only type available before the invention of the pneumatic tyre in the second half of the 19th century, and this type of cart is often still the most popular in countries where there is a long tradition of cart building. Solid-tyred wheels can be made of wood or steel. The tyre may be a piece of rubber or steel strip fitted over the rim, or the "tyre" may simply be the wooden or steel rim itself. An inherent characteristic of solid-tyred wheels is that they absorb very little of the shock loads imposed on the cart in use. The frame and wheels of carts of this type are therefore usually of relatively heavy construction to withstand these shock loads.

The details of design and construction vary widely according to local needs and traditions. Several examples of Asian carts made largely from wood and bamboo with traditional, large diameter, spoked wooden wheels are illustrated in Figures 2.1, 2.2 and 2.3. The dead weight of such wooden carts varies between about 250 and 400kg, and the payload of the cargo-carrying type drawn by a pair of bullocks is typically up to about 1,000kg. The timber used in traditional Asian carts is becoming increasingly expensive, and some research efforts have been directed at reducing both the weight and cost of large diameter wheels while retaining their performance characteristics. One promising approach being tried experimentally in India and Sri Lanka is to make large diameter wheels in steel with tensioned spokes (the same principle employed on bicycle wheels).

Figure 2.4 shows a wooden cart with wooden spoked wheels from Africa. The small diameter, and method of construction, of the wheel are typical of wooden wheels made in Africa, where there is a general lack of traditional skills in wheel building. As an alternative Figure 2.5 shows the use of a welded-steel spoked wheel on an African cart. Carts of the type illustrated with small, solid-tyred wheels are of fairly heavy construction, but have a low payload. The small wheels (650-800mm diameter) significantly increase both rolling resistance and the effect of bumpy terrain compared with the large diameter (1,100-1,500mm) Asian type.

Two-wheeled carts with pneumatic-tyred wheels

Pneumatic tyres have been used on animal carts since the 1930's in India when the Dunlop company introduced its "animal-drawn vehicle" (ADV) wheel/axle assembly. These ADV carts are more expensive than traditional carts, but are able to carry greater loads. A major intention of their introduction was to reduce the amount of damage caused to roads by carts with narrow, solid-tyred wheels. In 1979 Dunlop estimated that there were about 600,000 pneumatic-tyred carts in India: an impressive number but nevertheless only a small proportion of the total of about 15 million carts in the country. (3) The main constraint on the numbers sold has always been the relatively high cost of the ADV assembly compared with traditional wooden spoked wheels made by the village carpenter.[1] They appear to be most used in situations where full advantage can be taken of their greater load capacity, and the relatively high initial cost can be justified - for example, commercial operation in urban centres, bulk transport of crops such as sugar cane, and in prosperous agricultural areas. (3) These are also the circumstances where an operator can most easily obtain a loan to purchase an ADV cart.

India is the only country which has produced pneumatic tyres designed specifically for animal-drawn carts. However two-wheeled carts using motor vehicle tyres are widely used elsewhere in Asia and Africa. Two different types are shown in Figures 2.6 and 2.7.

In order to achieve the benefits of pneumatic tyres at lower cost than using an ADV assembly, many traditional carts have been converted, and new carts constructed, using complete axle assemblies from scrap motor vehicles. This approach is certainly effective, although such axle assemblies are unnecessarily heavy in this application. However, its widespread application is limited by the availability of suitable axles. While the axles may be available easily and cheaply in small

---

1. There are now indications that, in some parts of India, the cost advantage of the traditional, wooden spoked wheel is diminishing as good quality timber becomes more scarce and its price rises.

quantities, they are likely to become scarce and expensive if demand increases. Since the axles are likely to come from a variety of sources fitted with different sizes of wheel, there may also be difficulty in obtaining suitable tyres and inner tubes, both for the original carts and for replacement parts.

Organisations in a number of countries now manufacture wheel/axle assemblies, fitted with standard motor vehicle wheels and tyres (new or second-hand), specifically for animal carts. These may be sold as complete carts, or they may be supplied separately for other enterprises to add a body and hitching arrangement.

Figure 2.8 shows an unusual type of pneumatic-tyred cart using motor cycle wheels. It is a cheap, light duty cart with low payload, but can also be used as a hand cart.

Weights and payloads for conventional pneumatic-tyred carts vary considerably, as the data in Table 2.1, drawn from a variety of sources, shows. In general pneumatic-tyred carts are considered to be more efficient than carts with solid-tyred wheels, with lower rolling resistance on most types of terrain. All other things being equal, pneumatic-tyred carts would therefore be expected to have a higher payload than the solid-tyred type. However because of the large number of variables associated with the carts, draught animals and terrain, and because only a limited amount of experimental and theoretical work has been carried out, it is not possible to provide accurate data on tractive effort for different types of cart over a range of route conditions. The Annex discusses the theoretical aspects of tractive effort in detail, and some figures extracted from there are quoted in Table 2.2. These provide some insights but do not correlate well. Because the shock-absorbing properties of pneumatic tyres reduce the loads imposed on a cart, a lighter form of construction can be adopted than when solid-tyred wheels are used. The shock absorption by the pneumatic tyre also improves ride comfort for passengers and is beneficial to the draught animals. The major advantages of the solid-tyred type are ease of manufacture, low initial cost, and simplicity and ease of maintenance.

Note that the tractive effort for carts with pneumatic tyres will be significantly dependent on the inflation pressure of the tyres. A value often quoted for low speed, pneumatic tyred vehicles on good bitumen surfaces is $(5 + \frac{150}{p})$ kgf/tonne, where p is the inflation pressure of the tyre in p.s.i. (lbf/sq.in), so that on firm surfaces it is desirable to keep the tyres inflated to the manufacturer's recommendations. Little data is available on the influence of road roughness on tractive effort but it seems advisable to increase the above expression by a factor of 2 i.e. $(10 + \frac{300}{p})$ kgf/tonne for pneumatic tyred carts on rough bitumen roads.

On soft earth and sand surfaces a <u>low</u> inflation pressure is desirable to maximise the contact area of the tyre with the ground i.e. to spread the load. Therefore to minimise the tractive effort of carts on these surfaces the inflation pressure of the tyre should be kept as low as possible commensurate with its ability to support the load of

TABLE 2.1: WEIGHT AND USEFUL PAYLOAD OF TWO-WHEELED, PNEUMATIC-TYRED CARTS

	Weight (kg)	Payload (kg)
ADV Cart – India	400–500	2,500–3,000
Donkey Cart – Senegal	108	500
Horse Cart – Senegal	190	1,000
Bullock Cart – Vietnam	300	1,200–1,500
Horse Cart – Vietnam	250	800–900
Large Cart – China	700	2,000
Medium Cart – China	300	1,500

TABLE 2.2: TRACTIVE EFFORT FOR TWO-WHEELED CARTS

Type of Cart	Route	Specific Tractive Effort (kgf/tonne)	Reference
Steel-tyred wood wheels (150cm dia)	Tar road	58	6
	Dry earth road	84	6
	Grassy terrain	132	6
Pneumatic-tyred wheels (70cm dia)	Dry earth road	75	6
	Grassy terrain	180	6
Steel-tyred wooden wheels (122cm dia)	15cm deep dry sand (rutted)	173	7
	15cm deep dry soil (rutted)	100	7
	15cm deep wet soil (rutted)	160	7
	Concrete	28	7
Pneumatic-tyred wheels (80cm dia)	15cm deep dry sand (rutted)	81	7
	15cm deep dry soil (rutted)	28	7
	15cm deep wet soil (rutted)	142	7
	Concrete	22	7
Steel-tyred wheels	Ploughed land	136	8
	Earth road	21	8
Pneumatic-tyred wheels	Ploughed land	42	8
	Earth road	17	8
Wooden wheels (122cm dia, cast-iron bush bearing)	Earth road	31	9
	Paved road	15	9

the cart.

Tool carriers

In some countries multi-purpose animal-drawn tool carriers have been introduced for agricultural use. Many of these are fitted with two pneumatic-tyred wheels and can be converted into a cart using special attachments. The resulting vehicle is certainly useful, although if a cart is required frequently the time necessary to convert the tool carrier may be a significant disadvantage. Converted tool carriers do not make very efficient carts because they are heavy, and certain undesirable compromises have to be made to provide for multi-purpose use. As a result tool carrier carts usually have low ground clearance and a high load platform. The example shown in Figure 2.9 has a stated payload of up to 1,000kg.

2.2.2 Four-Wheeled Carts

Four-wheeled farm waggons and passenger coaches were very common in Europe and North America before the advent of the motor vehicle. Their main advantages over two-wheeled carts, then as now, are inherent stability and large load capacity. The construction of a four-wheeled cart is relatively complex, as a steering mechanism is necessary and the construction must either be very strong, or some form of suspension must be incorporated in order to withstand the twisting forces imposed on the vehicle as it traverses rough ground. These requirements, combined with the need for four wheels, add considerably to the cost and weight of construction. Four-wheeled carts are certainly heavier, more complex, expensive and difficult to manoeuvre than the two-wheeled variety. While it is feasible for one animal to haul a small four-wheeled cart, these vehicles are more usually drawn by teams of two or more.

Historically, four-wheeled carts were made almost entirely of wood, and a great deal of experience and skill was necessary to create a satisfactory vehicle. Numerous historical publications describe the construction and use of European coaches and waggons (1, 2, 10) but their complexity is such that they are unlikely to be reproduced in this form today. However four-wheeled carts are used today in Asia and Africa, though they are much less common than the two-wheeled type.

Modern materials make the construction of four-wheeled carts much simpler. Nearly all modern carts have pneumatic tyres and use steel for the load-bearing parts of the structure. Little information is available about tractive effort requirements, but it would appear that four-wheeled carts are most useful on smooth, hard and relatively flat surfaces. In China, loads of 3,000-4,000kg are carried on four-wheeled carts, and six-wheeled carts (four wheels on the rear axle) also exist, carrying up to 8,000kg (5). A small four-wheeled cart is shown in Figure 2.10.

A variation of the normal four-wheeled cart is the adjustable length cart. This is built in two separate parts with a steering axle and hitching arrangement on one part and a non-steering axle on the other. The two parts are fixed to opposite ends of a long rigid load such as timber or lengths of steel (Figure 2.11).

An advantage of four-wheeled carts is that they are self-supporting, and do not impose any vertical loads on the draught animals. Thus the whole of the animal's effort can be devoted to hauling the cart. Experiments have also been made in India with a three-wheeled cart. This is based on a two-wheeled layout but with a third, pivoting wheel attached at the front. The aim of this design is to achieve the advantages of a four-wheeled cart, but without the additional cost and complexity. However the work has not been taken beyond the experimental stage.

2.3 Animal Draught

2.3.1 Animals

Types of animal

A variety of animals are used for pulling carts in different parts of the world. The two most common types, bovines and equines, are considered here together with the camel, which is used in many arid areas.

The <u>bovine</u> or <u>ox</u> family includes bullocks (castrated males); cows (females) and buffaloes (bulls are not generally used for draught purposes). The bovine family includes many different species, but they will be referred to here collectively as <u>oxen</u>.[1]

The <u>equine</u> or <u>horse</u> family includes horses; ponies (small horses); donkeys and mules (donkey/horse half breeds). Horses and donkeys are sufficiently different to merit separate consideration.[1]

There are two species of <u>camel</u>, but only one of them, the Arabian or dromedary which has one hump, is common in the arid regions of Africa and the Indian sub-continent. The two-humped Bactrian camel is found mainly in the colder regions of west Asia.

Performance of animals

The cart hauling performance of draught animals is most usefully defined in terms of the tractive effort (or draught force) which they can apply. Tractive power (or rate of work), the product of tractive effort and working speed, is a less useful definition because, unlike a motor vehicle, the power of a draught animal cannot be applied continuously and indefinitely. Also, since most animals tend to adopt similar working speeds, tractive power tends to be proportional to tractive effort. More important performance characteristics are maximum instantaneous effort and length of working time per day.

---

1. Detailed descriptions of the many species within these two groups are given in References 11 and 12.

Many factors affect the working performance of animals, including their weight and body type, physical condition, breed characteristics, temperament, management and the climate. Figure 2.12 illustrates the relationship between these and other factors. All these vary according to local circumstances, and this variation is reflected in the results of the numerous tests which have been carried out to determine the work output of animals. However, useful guidelines can be given to allow reasonable estimates of performance to be made.

For pulling carts it is the sustainable tractive effort which an animal can generate that is of most interest. This is primarily dependent on body weight as shown in Table 2.3. Gowen (13) compares results from a variety of sources which are in reasonable agreement about sustainable tractive effort.

In general, most animals can exert a draught force of 10-14% of their body weight when working at speeds of 2.5 to 4km/hr. However, donkeys produce rather more at 15-20%. Estimates of body weight vary considerably but those given in Table 2.3 are reasonably typical.

The normal speed of work is similar for all animals at 3-4km/hr, though one would normally expect equines to travel slightly faster than bovines since the latter are naturally slow-moving animals. However horses and ponies work at much higher speeds than the above (see earlier reference (1) to pre-20th century English mail coaches). However this can only be achieved by a significant reduction in the tractive effort and/or the duration of the working period.

An important characteristic of draught animals is that, over a short period of time, they can exert considerably more than the sustainable tractive effort. This is particularly relevant in pulling carts because a significantly higher force is needed to set a wheeled vehicle in motion than to keep it rolling. It is also useful in climbing short gradients and in traversing bumps and potholes. There is little data available about the maximum instantaneous effort exerted by different animals, but a comparison of test results that do exist indicates that bovines can produce a short term effort of 100% of their body weight, whilst equines are rather better at 130-200% (13).

If the tractive effort required to pull a cart exceeds the capability of a single animal a team of two or more can be used. When animals are hitched in teams the useful effort available per animal is rather less than that produced by an animal on its own. The reduction in effort produced per animal amounts to 7.5% for a team of two, 15% for three, 22% for four, 30% for five and 37% for six (11). It is common practice to use one or two animals to pull a cart, much less so three or more. The number of animals used will be conditioned by the need to provide adequate total tractive effort, by traditional practices, and by other uses of the draught animals, for example in agriculture.

---

1. A detailed analysis of tractive effort produced by different breeds of African cattle is contained in Reference 14.

TABLE 2.3: ESTIMATES OF TRACTIVE EFFORT PRODUCED BY DIFFERENT ANIMALS AT LOW AND HIGH SPEEDS

Type of Animal	Mature Weight (kg)	Low Speed		High Speed	
		Speed (km/hr)	Draft (kgf)	Speed (km/hr)	Draft (kgf)
Horse					
light	385	2.4	48	4.0	39
medium	500	2.4	63	4.0	50
heavy	850	2.4	106	4.0	85
Mule					
light	200	2.4	32	4.0	20
heavy	600	2.4	96	4.0	60
Donkey					
light	190	2.4	30	4.0	19
heavy	300	2.4	48	4.0	30
Ox					
light	210	2.4	30	4.0	21
medium	450	2.4	64	4.0	45
heavy	900	2.4	129	4.0	90
Cow					
light	200	2.4	20	3.5	16
heavy	575	2.4	58	3.5	48
Buffalo					
light	400	2.4	56	3.2	40
medium	650	2.4	91	3.2	65
heavy	900	2.4	126	3.2	90
Camel (dromedary)					
light	370	3.5	50	4.0	37
heavy	600	3.5	84	4.0	60

Source: Goe and McDowell (11)

However it is desirable, in most circumstances, to limit the capacity of the cart to suit a maximum of two animals. With more than two the time and cost of caring for the animals increases, the hitching and harnessing arrangements are more complex, control is more difficult, and efficiency decreases significantly.

The length of time for which animals will sustain their normal tractive effort is important in determining their effectiveness as a power source for transport. Again there is considerable variation in the data from different sources, but the following figures are suggested as reasonable guidelines: oxen 4-6hr/day; horses 6-8hr/day;

donkeys 3-4hr/day; mules 6-8hr/day; camels 6-8hr/day. In practice it is unlikely that animals will be worked continuously for such periods, since rest periods will usually occur in the course of the working day. If water buffaloes are used a specific consideration is that they need to be taken to wallow regularly.

2.3.2 Harnessing and Hitching Arrangements

There are many ways of attaching an animal to a cart, which vary according to the type and number of animals used, the type of cart, and local tradition. There are two parts to the attachment – the harness to which the animal applies its force directly, and the hitch which transfers the force from the harness to the cart. Both parts are important in determining the effectiveness with which the animal's effort is used in hauling the cart.

Bovine harnesses

The most common type of harness for oxen is the shoulder yoke. For two animals this consists of a strong horizontal beam which sits on the animals' necks, and attaches in the centre to a single drawpole on the cart (Figures 2.13 and 2.14). For a single animal a curved, or 'V'-shaped yoke is used which is attached to the cart by two shafts, one on either side of the animal, as shown in Figure 2.7. Shoulder yokes usually have retaining straps, ropes or bars fitted under the animals' necks. The shoulder yoke is cheap, simple and robust, but it has a number of disadvantages:

- it does not utilise efficiently the strength in the animal's legs, shoulder and back;

- the vertical loads of a two-wheeled cart are supported on the animal's neck;

- the restraining strap can press against the animal's neck;

- there is only a small area of contact between the yoke and the animal's neck. The yoke tends to rub and chafe, causing sores and wounds.

Head yokes are also used in some parts of the world with short-necked oxen. The yoke is again a horizontal beam but is tied to the head(s) of the animal(s). Like the shoulder yoke the head yoke is very cheap, simple and robust. However it also shares the disadvantages of being both inefficient and harmful to the animals. The problems of these traditional yokes are very significant in reducing both the productive work output of the animals and their useful working lives, and there is a strong case for introducing improved harnessing methods for bovines.

A simple improvement is to add padding to the traditional type of shoulder yoke (Figure 2.15). This increases the area over which the loads are applied to the animal(s) and provides some protection from injury. A more comprehensive improvement is the three-pad collar harness, originally introduced in Europe in the 1930's (Figure 2.16(a)). This collar allows the animal to apply its power effectively through the shoulders and to move freely, while the three pads spread the load over a large area and protect from injuries. (Note that the three-pad arrangement is used for a bovine because a full collar would impede its wind pipe). The three-pad collar can be expensive, but Figure 2.16(b) illustrates an approach to reducing cost, by using naturally-shaped hardwood for the frame, and local materials for the padding.

It is important to note that, in situations where the shoulder or head yokes are traditionally used, a significant effort is likely to be needed to demonstrate the benefits of more effective, but possibly more expensive, harnesses, and to train animals and handlers to adapt to new methods.

Equine harnesses

Two types of harness are commonly used on equines, the breastband for light duty work, and the full collar for heavy duty. The breastband harness consists of a broad strap which passes around the animal's chest, to which the draught force is applied, and an adjustable shoulder strap to hold the breastband in position (Figures 2.17 and 2.20). The full collar harness is rather more complex but consists essentially of a padded collar, reinforced with metal 'hames', which fits right around the animal's neck as shown in Figure 2.18. Because their physiology is different from bovines, equines can wear full collars which pass around the front of the neck. Both types of equine harness are effective, comfortable for the animals, and suitable for hauling carts, though the collar is preferable for heavy-duty work. However a full-collar harnessing system with the various hitching straps, made from leather which is the best material, can be very expensive. Cost can be reduced by using materials which are easily available locally, for example suitably-shaped timber for the hames and vegetal matter to make the collar or padding.

More detailed information on bovine and equine harnessing, including a range of designs, is contained in Reference 15.

Camel harnesses

Figure 2.19 illustrates a typical camel harnessing arrangement. The draught force is applied through a saddle over the camel's hump which, for a two-wheeled cart, would also support the vertical load. An alternative method is to apply the draught force through a strap passing over the camel's neck directly in front of the hump.

Hitching of a single animal

The hitching arrangement depends on the type of cart, the number of animals and the type of harness used. A cart to be pulled by one animal is fitted with two shafts, one either side of the animal (Figure 2.7). Carts to be pulled by two or more animals are normally fitted with a single central drawpole to which the animals are attached on either side (see Figure 2.2). On a two-wheeled cart the shafts or drawpole must transmit the vertical force to balance the cart as well as the horizontal pulling force. They are therefore fixed rigidly to the cart and often form an integral part of the structure. On a four-wheeled cart the shafts or drawpole are not required to transmit a vertical force but must allow the animals to move up and down relative to the cart. They are attached to the cart with a hinge which allows this vertical movement. An example is shown in Figure 2.19.

For two-wheeled carts drawn by a single horse or donkey the standard practice is for the vertical load to be supported on the animal's back. The animal wears a saddle, which may consist simply of a broad belt over the back with a belly strap to hold it in place, as in Figure 2.3 and Figure 2.20. The shafts rest on loops in the saddle straps and are tied to the harness to transmit the pulling force. A braking force can be applied by using a breech strap which is fixed to the shafts and passes behind the animal (Figure 2.20). Many bovines will not accept a load on their back. Therefore, for a cart drawn by a single bovine it is standard practice for the cart shafts to be attached directly to the harness. This means that the vertical loads are taken on the neck. For bovines that will accept a load on their back a saddle arrangement, as for equines, is preferable (Figure 2.21). It is not traditional practice to fit a breeching strap with bovines, but there is no reason why it should not be done, as it provides an acceptable braking arrangement at minimal cost.

Hitching of more than one animal

The method of hitching of two animals to a cart with a central drawpole depends on the type of harness used. An oxen shoulder (or head) yoke is attached to a drawpole via a hitching point at its centre (Figure 2.13). The yoke can be simply tied to the drawpole, but it is preferable if it can pivot (about the drawpole axis) to allow for different sizes of animal. It is possible, and desirable, to fit breech straps to provide a braking force, but the vertical load of a two-wheeled cart must be applied through the yoke.

Where the two animals are harnessed independently, most commonly equines with breastbands or collars, the hitching arrangement to the drawpole cart is more complicated. Two traces are attached to the harness of each animal; one on each side, and then to a spreader bar at the rear of each animal. The spreader bars are connected to an evener which is fitted at its centre to the drawpole (Figure 2.22(a)). The front of the drawpole must also be attached to the animals to enable them to support the vertical load (two-wheeled carts only) and to provide a braking force. There are three possible methods of doing this as shown in Figure 2.22. The first method is simplest, but the second keeps the collar better located. The third method is preferred because the vertical and control forces are applied directly to saddle and breech straps, rather than to the main harness.

As the above discussion illustrates, the hitching of two or more independently-harnessed animals to a cart can become very complex.

There is an alternative method by which several animals can be hitched to a cart fitted with two shafts. This method, which is widely used in China, is both simple and flexible, and there is considerable potential for its use elsewhere. The first animal is hitched between the shafts in the normal way for a single animal, and both supports the vertical load of the cart and also provides a pulling force. One or more additional animals can be hitched by traces directly to the cart, and provide draught forces only. Figure 2.23 shows three horses hitched to a cart by this method. A feature of the method is that it allows animals of different sizes, breeds or species to be used together, and young animals can be trained by hitching them alongside more experienced ones. However as one animal provides all the braking force, this method should be used with caution where gradients have to be negotiated, unless a mechanical brake is fitted.

2.4 Bodywork

The type of bodywork fitted to a cart usually has only a limited influence on its technical performance as measured, for example, by draught requirements. Further it is only in certain specialised applications that the type of bodywork used will affect the specification of the overall configuration, structure and wheel/axle assembly of the cart, though it may well influence their dimensions. However the type of bodywork fitted will have a major effect on the practicality and convenience of the cart in a particular application. The specification of the bodywork is therefore of crucial importance in determining the popularity, usefulness and economic efficiency of a cart design. A cart manufacturer may well offer for sale a general purpose cart, together with several special purpose adaptations of the same basic design.

2.4.1 General Purpose Bodywork

The majority of carts, particularly those owned by rural families, are used for a variety of purposes, including the carrying of passengers and a range of different cargoes. For such applications general purpose bodywork is appropriate. The simplest, cheapest and lightest type of general purpose bodywork is a flat platform (Figure 2.24). Passengers can simply sit on the platform, and the arrangement is adequate for carrying sacks, drums and other cargoes that are in some form of container. It is preferable if the load is tied down. The simplest type of cart is one in which the full width axle is attached to a flat platform by means of two spacers. The height of the platform is set so that a straight drawpole or pair of shafts can run forward to the animal(s). While this arrangement is simple it has the disadvantage that the load platform is higher than necessary, which reduces the stability of the cart, and can make loading difficult. To lower the height of the load platform requires a more complex arrangement for the drawpole or shafts and, in the case of a large-wheeled cart, of the axle. The flat platform can be built in wood, in steel or in a combination of the two (i.e. a platform with a steel frame and wooden decking). In Asia many ox carts have a platform and drawpole made from lengths of bamboo lashed together.

The addition of sides to the platform is useful for constraining long loads such as timber, bamboo and sugar cane (Figure 2.2 shows an extreme example of this). An open topped box body, a platform with sides, frontboard and tailboard, allows loose loads such as earth, sand or agricultural produce to be carried, and is also convenient for carrying packaged goods without tying them down (Figure 2.25). However the goods have to be lifted over the box for loading or unloading. It is therefore common practice to have a removable tailboard, or for the tailboard and sometimes the sides to be hinged so that they can be lowered for loading and unloading. However the hingeing and latching mechanisms increase both cost and complexity and, with repeated use, can be a source of maintenance problems. A seat for the driver and one or two passengers is sometimes provided at the front of the cart. However on a two-wheeled cart it is important to distribute the load to minimise the vertical force imposed on the draught animal(s). It may therefore be preferable to distribute any passengers (and the driver) to balance the load rather than to concentrate their weight at the front of the cart. An alternative method of providing for passengers is to fit bench seats on top of the side walls (Figure 2.26).

It is common practice for carts to be sold with no bodywork, or with only a flat platform fitted, so that the purchaser can arrange the construction or adaptation of the body to suit individual requirements. The making of the body can be done by a village carpenter, or by the purchaser, and this approach provides flexibility and helps to reduce the cost of the cart.

2.4.2 Special Purpose Bodywork

Special purpose bodywork is required on carts which are purchased for a specific application (e.g. construction work) or to provide a commercial transport service carrying particular types of load (e.g. passenger carrying or water delivery). The fitting of special purpose bodywork will normally increase the cost of a cart compared with a simple general purpose design. It is not possible to cover all types of body here, since it is feasible to develop an appropriate design for any specialised application. The examples below cover the more important uses of carts.

Passenger carrying

Historically a variety of two- and four-wheeled animal-drawn vehicles were used in Europe and America, many elaborately constructed with suspensions and waterproof compartments for comfort. Such vehicles, which were primarily the preserve of the rich, are no longer built, nor are they directly relevant to developing country requirements. Figure 2.3 illustrates a horse-drawn passenger cart typical of those found in a number of Asian countries. It illustrates the main features likely to be provided in a passenger body:

- bench seats, which may be padded, mounted along or across the body;

- either a low floor height or steps to facilitate entry and exit;

- a canopy for protection from sun and rain;

- sprung suspension for passenger comfort;

- provision for carrying the passengers' accompanying goods.

Ambulance

In effect a specialised form of passenger-carrying vehicle, a rural ambulance adaptation of an ox-cart has been tried experimentally in India. It has sprung suspension and weather protection and is designed to carry a full-length stretcher.

Water carrier

The simplest form of water carrier consists of one or more 200 litre drums with a filling spout at the top and a tap at the bottom, fixed to an otherwise standard flat platform cart. Better performance and lower cost may be achieved by building the cart specifically for this purpose. An example is shown in Figure 2.27, the water tank being mounted in a purpose-designed frame.

Water bowser

A particular type of water carrier is the water bowser, which is designed to sprinkle water on to the road surface as part of construction operations. This can also be made with 200 litre drums, as in Figure 2.28, or it may have a purpose-built tank.

Tipping cart

When moving large quantities of loose materials, for example on a construction site, a great deal of time can be saved by using a cart which will tip to unload, as shown in Figure 2.29. The cart must have a hinged or removable tailboard, and a robust tipping mechanism is essential for satisfactory operation. The platform of the cart must be relatively high off the ground to give a sufficient angle of tip to ensure that the material is fully discharged.

Bottom-dumping cart

An alternative to the tipping cart is the hopper cart. The base of the cart is made so that it can be opened and the load is discharged underneath. Figure 2.30 shows an example where the base is made in several sections, each of which pivots. This type has the advantages of a lower load platform and allows quicker unloading than a tipping cart, but the construction is complicated.

Stake-sided cart

Used for carrying bulky, low density loads such as hay, animal fodder etc. (Figure 2.31). The stake sides can be made to attach to a general-purpose platform cart.

2.5 Wheel/Axle Assembly

Technically the most complex element of a cart is the wheel/axle assembly or assemblies. This is likely to constitute the major part of the cost of the cart, and the types of wheel, tyre, axle and bearings used have a major influence on the overall characteristics of the complete vehicle.

2.5.1 Wheel and Tyre

The relative characteristics of solid- and pneumatic-tyred wheels have already been referred to in the discussion on two-wheeled carts. Pneumatic tyres provide a degree of shock absorption, improve ride comfort, allow lighter weight construction to be adopted and, under many operating conditions, are more efficient. However, they are also prone to punctures and, for reasons of low cost, availability and ease of maintenance solid-tyred wheels may be preferred.

Wooden wheels

The simplest type of wheel is the solid wooden wheel. The circular section may be cut directly from a tree trunk, but it is more common to bolt several rectangular pieces together as shown in Figure 2.32. A large amount of wood is used, especially for a large diameter wheel, and the wheel will be very heavy. This method of construction is simple but is only likely to be useful where wood is very cheap and where wheelwright skills do not exist.

Spoked wooden wheels are much more common than solid wheels and are probably most widely used in India. A detailed survey of bullock cart wheels made in India in the 1940's identified two distinct types: the 'arm' type where three parallel pairs of spokes pass through the hub and are fixed to the rim at each end (Figure 2.1); and the 'spoke' type where between eight and sixteen radial spokes are wedged into the hub and the rim at each end (Figure 2.33). Neither appears to have any particular advantage over the other. Wheel diameters varied from 900 to 1800mm and most used a rim about 50mm wide (16). The wooden spoke and rim sections used for cargo-carrying bullock carts are heavy, but the spoked wheels used on passenger-carrying horse-drawn carts in Asia are often of slender, elegant construction. The 'spoke' type of wheel is the more common in other parts of the world. The traditional method of construction uses wood throughout, as shown in Figure 2.33, but various modifications using bolted joints have been proposed in recent years to simplify construction (see Figure 2.4) since the traditional method is complicated and relies heavily on the skill of the wheelwright. In Europe and America it was common practice to 'dish' wheels, as shown in Figure 2.34, which made them stronger against the side loads imposed on slopes and by the motion of the animal(s). It also made the construction of the wheel and axle even more complicated, and increased both rolling resistance and damage to roads (1, 2, 10). Dished wheels are not used in developing countries, nor does there appear to be any good reason for their adoption.

Although more complex, spoked wooden wheels have a much better strength-to-weight ratio than solid wooden wheels. A small diameter is stronger and cheaper, but a large diameter is desirable for low rolling resistance, so a compromise to suit local requirements must be chosen.

Spoked steel wheels

Spoked steel wheels of welded construction are used primarily in areas where traditional wheelwright skills do not exist. Most have a flat steel rim which is attached to the hub by between six and twelve solid spokes, welded at each end, as shown in Figure 2.35. Spokes can be flat or round section. Hub designs vary to suit different types of bearing. If round section spokes are used the outer spoke ends are usually attached to the rim centre line. The inner ends may all be attached on the hub centre line or may be positioned at opposite ends of the hub alternately. The latter method triangulates the wheels and so improves the strength against side loads. Such wheels are not difficult to build with basic workshop facilities, though some care is needed to produce them accurately. However they have a poor strength-to-weight ratio compared with equivalent wooden spoked wheels, and the material cost will usually be high, especially for large diameter wheels. They are also prone to fatigue cracking of the welds where the spokes join the rim. The load carrying capability depends on the specification of the materials used and also on the quality of construction. Another method of construction is to use a 'T' section rim with flat spokes welded on either side of the web. This appears to give a better strength-to-weight ratio (Figure 2.36).

The simple welded-steel spoked wheels of the type described above are not normally made in the large diameters common for wooden wheels because of problems of excessive weight and inadequate strength. Better results can be achieved by utilising more structurally efficient steel sections (e.g. hollow sections and tubes) for the rim and spokes. Another promising approach to making large diameter steel wheels is the "tension-spoked" design being developed in India and Sri Lanka (Figure 2.37). These wheels, made in similar dimensions to traditional wooden spoked weels, have a flat steel rim reinforced with steel rods and a large number (24 for the Sri Lankan design), of slender steel spokes, tensioned by a threaded attachment to the hub or rim. These wheels are designed on the same principles as bicycle wheels and the tensioning of the spokes gives a high strength-to-weight ratio. They have proved successful on an experimental basis but have not yet been widely adopted.

Solid tyres

Wooden or steel wheels of the type described above can be fitted with solid tyres.

Steel tyres made of flat strip are often fitted to the rim of wooden wheels (Figure 2.2). They protect the wooden rim from wear in use, and also add to the strength of the wheel. The tyre can either be nailed to the wooden wheel, or formed as a complete hoop and shrunk on to the wheel after heating. For steel wheels the steel rim will also act as the tyre.

Solid rubber tyres made from rubber strip can be fitted to wooden or steel wheels (Figure 2.1). They reduce the damage caused to roads by narrow wheels with steel rims or tyres and protect the wheel rim from wear. They also provide a degree of shock absorption, and in some circumstances may reduce rolling resistance. They are easily fitted and cheap, often being made by cutting strips from scrap motor vehicle tyres.

Pneumatic-tyred wheels

Although, as Figure 2.8 shows, bicycle-type spoked wheels can be used for light-duty carts, pneumatic-tyred carts normally use conventional motor vehicle wheels, the size selected depending on availability and load-carrying requirements. These wheels are built for the automotive industry in very large numbers with complex machinery, which produces a light, strong and high quality wheel. However these wheels are imported items in most developing countries and the cost, if purchased new, is high. The use of second-hand wheels is one means of reducing this but supplies can prove difficult to obtain or become expensive, particularly if a large number of a single size are required to produce a batch of carts. A conventional motor vehicle wheel has a complex rim section shape to allow the fitting of the tyre, and as a result can only be produced economically in large quantities by capital-intensive methods. However for cart applications a two piece, split-rim wheel can be used satisfactorily with conventional automotive tyres. This type of wheel can be fabricated with simple equipment from commonly available steel sections, and can therefore be made in small numbers at a reasonable cost. Load capacity and strength-to-weight ratio compare favourably with a conventional wheel at the low operating speeds of carts. An integral hub can be used and its design varied to suit different types of bearing. These wheels are not yet well established, but the results of experimental use are promising. An example is illustrated in Figures 2.38 and 2.39.

Standard automotive pneumatic tyres can be used on animal-drawn carts. Used tyres with a worn tread are quite satisfactory for use on carts as long as the structure of the tyre carcass is sound, and in many situations will offer a significant cost saving over new tyres. It is preferable to fit an inner tube inside the tyre, and essential if the split-rim wheel discussed above is used. The tyres made in India for ADV wheel/axle assemblies are designed specifically (in terms of materials, construction and tread pattern) to suit the requirements of animal-drawn carts rather than motor vehicles. One disadvantage of pneumatic tyres is that they are prone to puncture. However a variety of methods are now available to reduce the occurrence of punctures. (See, for instance, a forthcoming publication of I.T. Publications Ltd.).

2.5.2 Axle

The term axle is used here to describe the means by which the wheels are attached to the main structure of the cart.

In Europe carts had axles made entirely of wood until the early 19th century, but when suitable iron and steel became available it was quickly adopted for this purpose because of its greater strength and wear resistance. Initially only the ends of the axles, where the wheels were attached, were made of steel, but by the middle of the 19th century all-steel axles were being fitted (2). All the wooden carts in Vagh's extensive survey in India in the 1930's had steel axles. While it is still possible to find examples of wooden axles, the use of steel is now standard practice throughout the world.

The cart axle can be arranged in two ways:

- As a 'dead' axle which is fixed to the cart. The wheels rotate about the axle on bearings mounted in the wheel hubs.

- As a 'live' axle which is fixed to the wheels and rotates in bearings (usually arranged in plummer blocks) fixed to the cart.

Dead axle

The dead axle is much the more common arrangement and is stronger, but the live axle is easier to make and to fit. The most common form of dead axle runs the full width of the cart with a wheel attached at each end and acts as a structural member. This is a very simple method of constructing a cart. Such a dead axle is made most simply from a single piece of round section steel bar. This is suitable for the attachment of the wheels, but gives a poor strength-to-weight ratio in its structural role. It is more efficient to fabricate the axle with a structural (e.g. hollow, 'I' or channel) section used for the central portion and short lengths of round bar welded to each end for attaching the wheels.

There are two other forms of dead axle:

i) separate stub axles mounted on either side of the main cart structure, but not joined directly across the width of the cart. This requires a more complex cart structure, but provides greater flexibility in body design, since the height of the body platform is not constrained by the axle line;

ii) each wheel mounted independently on its own axle, with the structure of the cart arranged so that each axle is attached to the frame on both sides of the wheel (see Figure 2.2). This is a fairly complex method of construction which appears to offer no significant advantages.

Live axle

Live axles are usually arranged as two separate half-axles. Each half-axle carries one wheel and runs in two bearings mounted underneath the cart (see Figure 3.14). This allows the wheels to turn independently when the cart changes direction.

Motor vehicle axles

Motor vehicle axles are commonly used for animal carts. The typical method uses the rear axle from a rear-wheel-drive vehicle. The complete rear axle assembly will include the final drive and differential mechanism and two half shafts mounted inside the axle casing. Even if the unwanted parts of the final drive and differential are removed this remains a heavy axle assembly for use on an animal-drawn cart. However some types of front-wheel-drive motor vehicle are fitted with a dead rear axle - essentially a beam with a wheel hub mounting at each end - which is better suited to animal cart applications. With the increasing popularity of front-wheel-drive cars and light commercial vehicles such axles are becoming more easily available. An additional complexity of all motor vehicle axles is that the hubs, into which the bearings are fitted, are attached to the ends of the axles and the wheels are bolted on separately, so that the wheels can be removed easily to repair punctures. Motor vehicle axle assemblies will normally have brake mechanisms fitted which can be adapted to provide a braking system for the cart.

Axles for four-wheeled carts

A four-wheeled cart requires two different axles. At the rear a dead axle the same as that on a two-wheeled cart is used. However the front axle must include a steering mechanism. In the past European carts had the front axle mounted on a wide wooden beam. Another beam at the front of the cart rested on this, connected by a pivot pin in the centre. This was a simple, workable system but required considerable force to turn and was subject to rapid wear. The turning circle was also very large. Modern carts use two different types of steering:

 i) the swivelling bolster, where a normal wheel/axle assembly is fixed underneath a large diameter steel plate or ring, which rotates on a similar plate or ring fixed to the cart body;

 ii) axle-pivot steering where pivot pins are fitted to the ends of a fixed axle on which the wheels turn by means of a linkage.

Both types are illustrated in Figure 2.40. Swivelling-bolster steering is relatively simple and strong, and a small turning radius is possible. However it is also heavy and the front of the cart becomes less stable as the turning radius is decreased, which may cause the cart to tip on sloping ground or with a badly balanced load. Axle-pivot steering is relatively complicated and the turning radius is larger, but it is lighter and there are no stability problems. Swivelling bolsters are more commonly used for animal carts.

2.5.3 Bearings

The function of the bearings is to minimise friction as the wheels rotate. There are two main types used in carts: plain bearings, also known as bushes, which locate inside a housing and fit around the axle; and rolling element bearings in which the axle and housing are separated by balls or rollers which rotate as the wheel turns. A well lubricated and fitted plain bearing can have an acceptably low coefficient of friction. However they are frequently not well maintained or fitted, and they then generate considerably more friction. If the arrangement is well designed rolling element bearings need very little maintenance and generally are not as badly affected by neglect as plain bearings. Both types of bearing can be built into the wheel hub for a 'dead' axle, or fitted into a housing for a 'live' axle.

Plain bearings

Plain bearings used in animal carts are most commonly made of wood, cast iron, or steel pipe. Ideally the plain bearing should be a close fit around the axle. However on many of the traditional wooden carts in Asia the bearing is made as a loose fit over the axle. The most simple wooden bearing is a hole drilled through the centre of a wooden hub or housing. However it is preferable to fit a separate bearing which can be replaced as it wears, and can be made from an appropriate hardwood or "oil soaked" wood to minimise friction. Both cast iron and steel pipe can give reasonably low friction and wear rate. However it is difficult to seal plain bearings completely to prevent dirt or other abrasive particles from entering and increasing both friction and wear. Regular greasing helps to keep out dirt as well as reducing friction. The major advantage of plain bearings is that they can be made with widely available materials on a small scale, usually at relatively low cost.

Rolling element bearings

Rolling element bearings are made from high quality hardened steel to very fine tolerances and are produced in very large numbers to achieve a reasonable cost. Most developing countries import them and they are usually more expensive than plain bearings. However price depends to a large extent on the level of demand for a particular bearing. Cost can therefore be kept reasonably low by selecting a size and specification of bearing for which there is a large local demand. Rolling element bearings are always used in pairs and are more compact than plain bearings since load capacity is considerably greater for a given size. A variety of seals can be used to prevent dirt entering in different conditions. Some bearings are 'sealed for life' and require no maintenance. The simplest type of bearing consists of a set of spherical balls between an inner and outer ring which are located on the axle and in the bearing housing respectively. Greater load capacity is achieved by using cylindrical rollers instead of balls. Motor vehicle wheels invariably use bearings with tapered rollers, which can withstand considerable axial as well as radial loads. They can also be used on animal carts, although the rated capacity of motor vehicle bearings is often well in excess of requirements.

2.5.4 Suspension

Few animal carts today utilise any form of sprung suspension to reduce the magnitude of shock loads transmitted from the wheels to the cart body and the animal(s). They are sometimes used on modern carts with pneumatic tyres, most commonly where a motor vehicle axle is used and the original spring mounting is retained. The question of whether animal carts benefit significantly from the use of suspension has received little attention, so a definitive answer cannot be given. It is worth noting however that springs were a standard feature of European coaches in the past where they made a significant contribution to passenger comfort, but they were not used on heavier, four-wheeled agricultural wagons. Suspension will inevitably increase the cost of a cart and there is some evidence to suggest that for pneumatic-tyred carts the benefits do not outweigh the additional cost and complication. This is probably because at the slow speed at which animal carts operate pneumatic tyres provide sufficient suspension in themselves.

2.5.5 Brakes

Many carts do not have any form of braking system other than relying on the animals to slow and stop the cart. However, despite the additional cost any cart which is regularly used in hilly rather than flat terrain should incorporate brakes. This will improve safety, reduce the load on the animal(s) when going downhill and allow rest stops on the way up. The simplest and most common type of brake found on animal carts consists of a wooden or steel bar, sometimes with a brake shoe at each end, which can be pressed against the outside surface of the wheel when necessary. More complex systems have been proposed but are rarely used, though carts made with motor vehicle axles can often utilise the existing brake mechanism built into the hub.

The brakes on a cart can be locked to prevent it moving when parked, but a useful addition for a two-wheeled cart is a means of supporting it in a horizontal position. This allows the animal(s) to rest or be removed if required and also facilitates loading and unloading. The simplest parking mechanism consists of two lengths of wood placed under the front and rear of the cart.

2.6 Selection Method

This chapter provides the information necessary to prepare an overall specification of the most appropriate type of cart to suit a particular set of conditions. In order to do this it is necessary to define those features of the cart which are essential if it is to perform its required function given the conditions imposed by local geography, culture and availability of resources and skills. The selection method presented here consists of a set of key questions aimed at defining the essential features of a cart to suit local circumstances. By comparing the answers to these questions with the information on the characteristics of different cart elements presented in the previous sections of this chapter, an overall specification for an appropriate cart can be developed. In putting together a specification it is important to distinguish between those features which it is essential to incorporate and those which are only desirable. Both must be balanced against cost considerations.

Q1. What types of draught animal are used or available at present?

In most circumstances it is unlikely to be worthwhile introducing a new breed of draught animal to an area just to meet transport needs. There may sometimes be a case for introducing a new breed of animal to develop the use of animal draught in agriculture and in transport. However in general the selection should be restricted to the types of draught animal already in use in the area, and to animals which are owned locally and, with suitable training, could be adapted to draught work. Even if the available animals are not ideal for transport there are good reasons for preferring them. The local breeds will be well suited to climatic conditions and resistant to prevalent diseases, the necessary animal husbandry skills will already exist, and the cost of buying the animals locally should be relatively low. Also in many agricultural applications, the animals will be used for ploughing and other tasks as well as for transport. All these factors should outweigh any operational advantages which might be gained by introducing new types.

The type of animal and its weight will determine the tractive effort it will be able to produce and the length of time it will be able to work in a day. This will be a key factor in determining the payload that can be carried and the number of animals to be used, which will in turn affect the economics of operation. It may be necessary to decide whether it is preferable to use small carts drawn by a single animal or fewer larger carts drawn by a pair.

Q2. What will the cart be used for?

The types of goods to be carried, and the frequency and method of loading and unloading, will determine the type and size of bodywork required. The overall quantities of goods to be moved, and the amount which the cart must be capable of carrying in one trip, will determine the load capacity within the limitations imposed by other factors. If a cart is to be used intensively for one specific purpose the payload will have a significant effect on the economics of its operation and maximising this is likely to be a major objective, possibly to the extent of using a four-wheeled, rather than two-wheeled cart. For less intensive use, keeping the cost of the cart to a reasonable level may be more important than maximising payload.

Clearly the goods to be carried will influence the type of bodywork to be fitted to the cart, and if low-density loads are to be moved, the volume of the load space will be important. If passengers or delicate goods are to be carried frequently then pneumatic tyres or even suspension may be essential.

Q3. **What are the route conditions?**

The roughness and hardness of the typical route surfaces and the variation in conditions during the year, will also affect the tractive effort needed and will play a major part in deciding what type of wheels and tyres should be used. Local route conditions may also impose limitations on the dimensions of the cart, e.g. the track width or the ground clearance. The presence of gradients on local routes will have a significant influence on the cart design. Hilly terrain will require a fairly small, light cart relative to the number of draught animals, and will argue against the use of a four-wheeled cart. Brakes are likely to be essential if a cart is to be used regularly on inclines.

Q4. **What are the local market conditions?**

Local cultural and social preferences will often influence the specification of a cart in terms of selection of draught animals, appearance, materials to be used, or by imposing limitations on the use of carts. The availability of maintenance skills and facilities will influence many aspects of the design, including the specifications of wheels and bearings (e.g. can punctures be repaired; are sealed bearings worthwhile?) and decisions on whether to include complexities such as braking and suspension. Most important, the economic circumstances of local users are likely to impose cost constraints on the carts.

Figure 2.1 Two-wheeled cart with wooden spoked wheels and bamboo platform.
Note strip rubber tyres fitted to wheel rim: Bangladesh.

Figure 2.2

Two-wheeled cart with spoked wheels, constructed in wood. Bodywork is suitable for carrying long loads such as sugar cane or bamboo. Note that wheels are supported on both sides and are fitted with strip rubber tyres: Laos.

Figure 2.3 Two-wheeled passenger cart. Horse is hitched to cart with collar harness and saddle: Burma.

Figure 2.4 Two-wheeled wooden cart: Tanzania.

Figure 2.5 Two-wheeled cart with welded spoke steel wheels: United Republic of Tanzania.

Figure 2.6 Two-wheeled steel cart with pneumatic tyres: Botswana.

Figure 2.7 Wooden cart with pneumatic tyres and shoulder yoke for one animal: Indonesia.

Figure 2.8 Small two-wheeled wooden cart with pneumatic tyres, used also as a handcart: China.

Figure 2.9 Multi-purpose two-wheeled tool carrier with cart conversion: The Sudan.

Figure 2.10 Four-wheeled donkey cart: Botswana.

Figure 2.11 Four-wheeled adjustable length cart for
            carrying long, rigid loads: China.
            Source: Reference 5

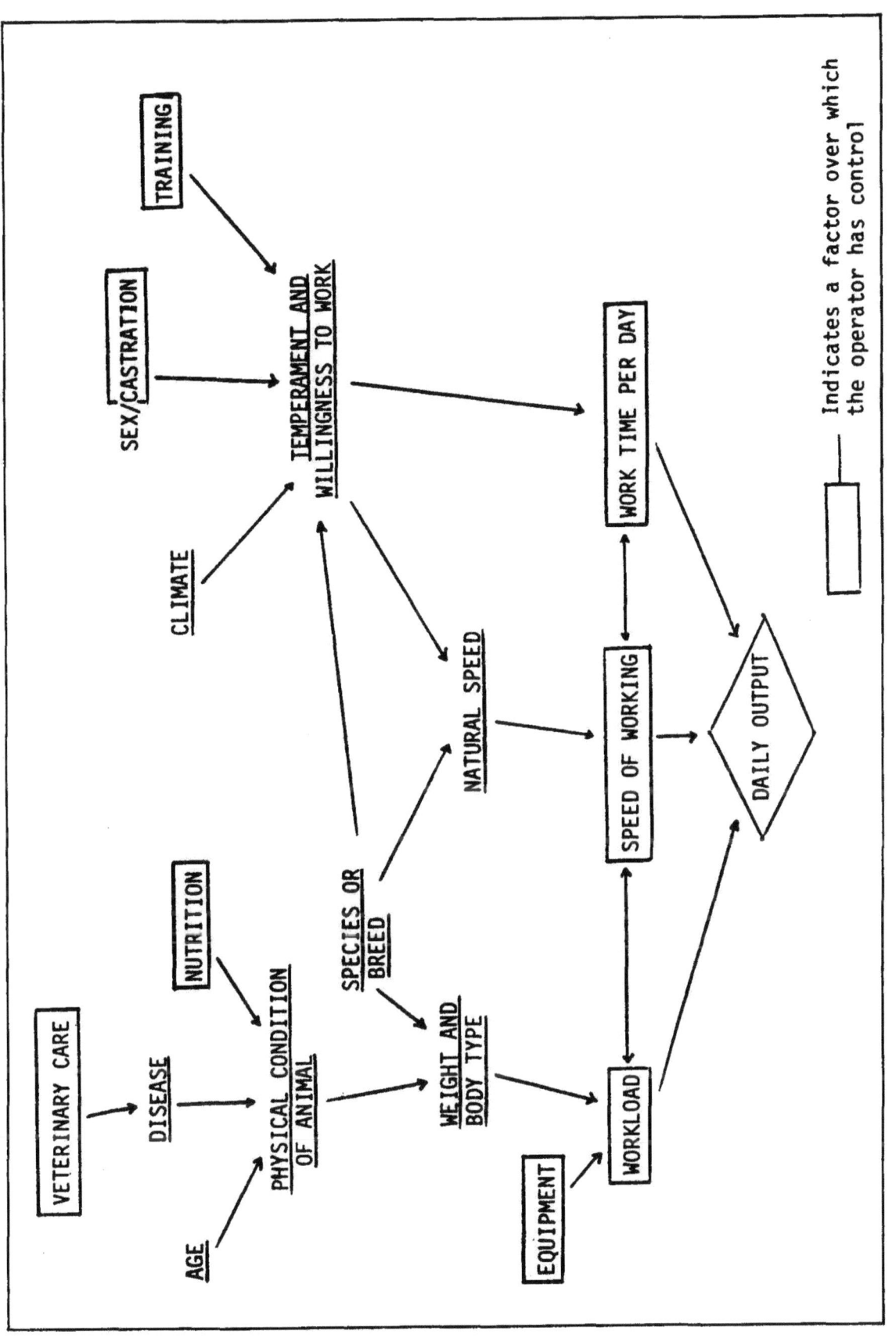

Figure 2.12 Factors affecting tractive effort of animals.
Source: Gowen (13)

Figure 2.13 Bamboo shoulder yoke for two oxen: Bangladesh.

Figure 2.14 Steel shoulder yoke for two oxen: Lesotho.

Figure 2.15 Traditional neck yoke, improved with additional padding: Sudan.

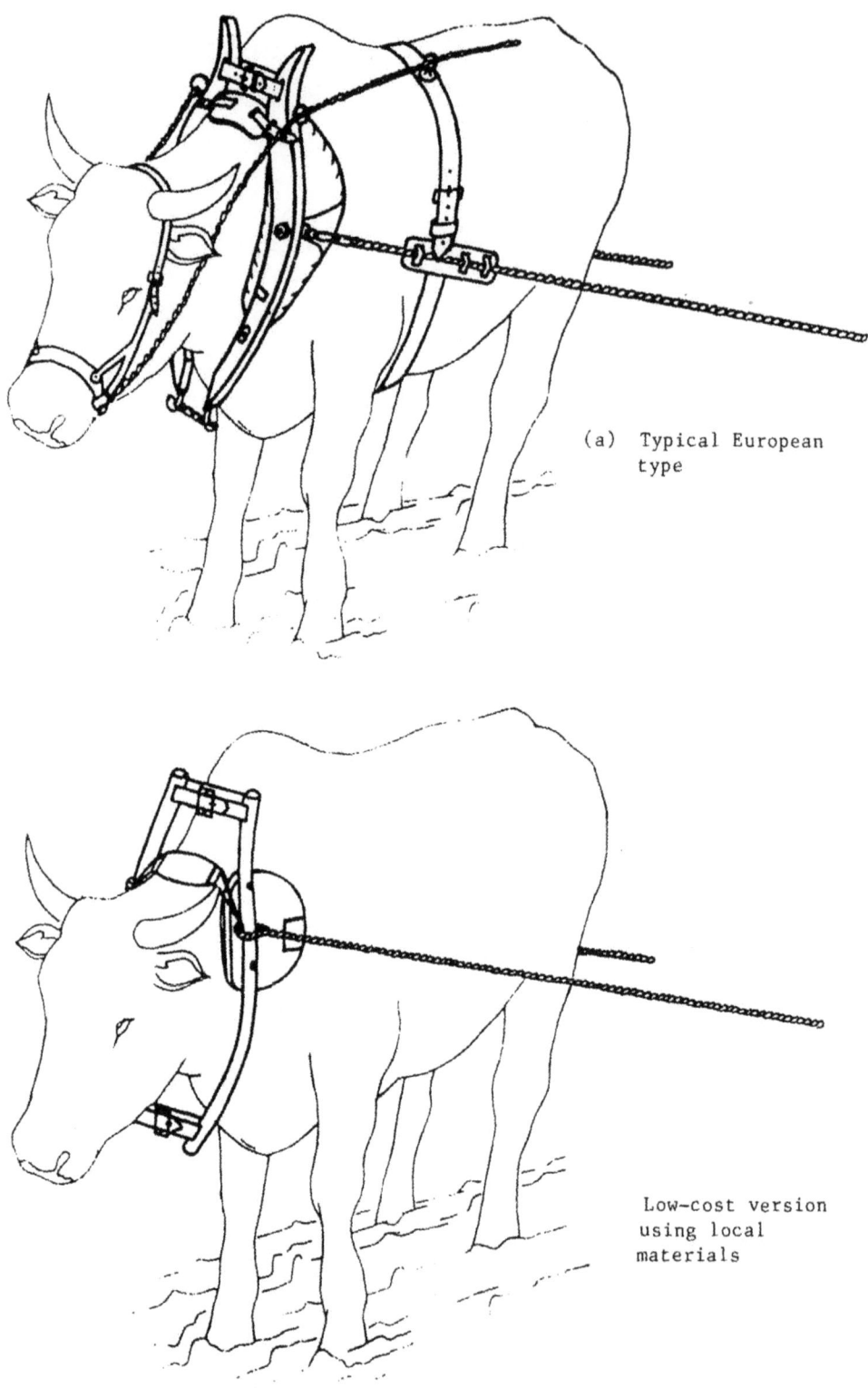

(a) Typical European type

Low-cost version using local materials

Figure 2.16 Three-pad collar harnesses for bovines.

Figure 2.17 A breastband harness.

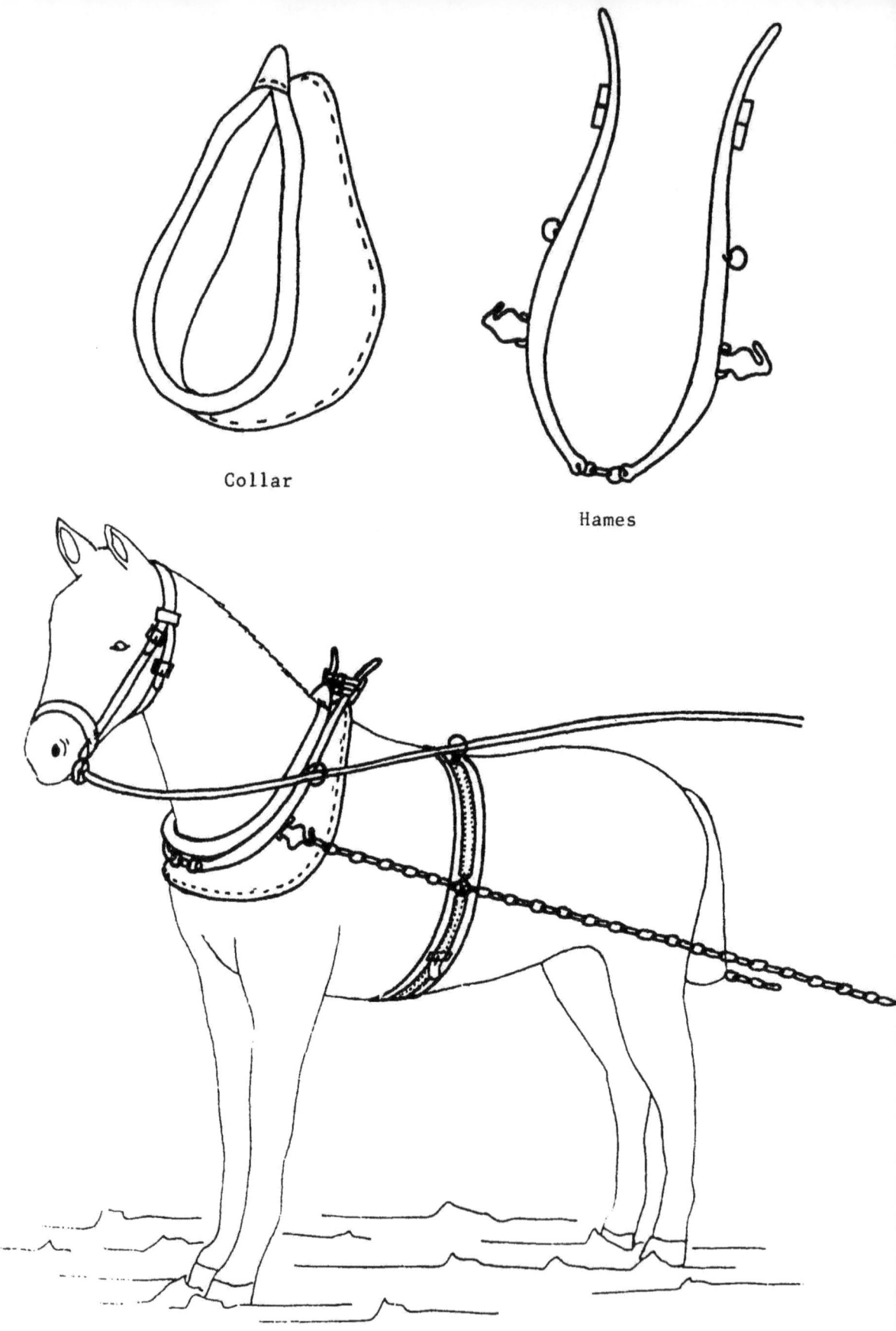

Figure 2.18 A full collar harness.

Figure 2.19 Camel harness and hitching arrangement for a four-wheeled cart: India.

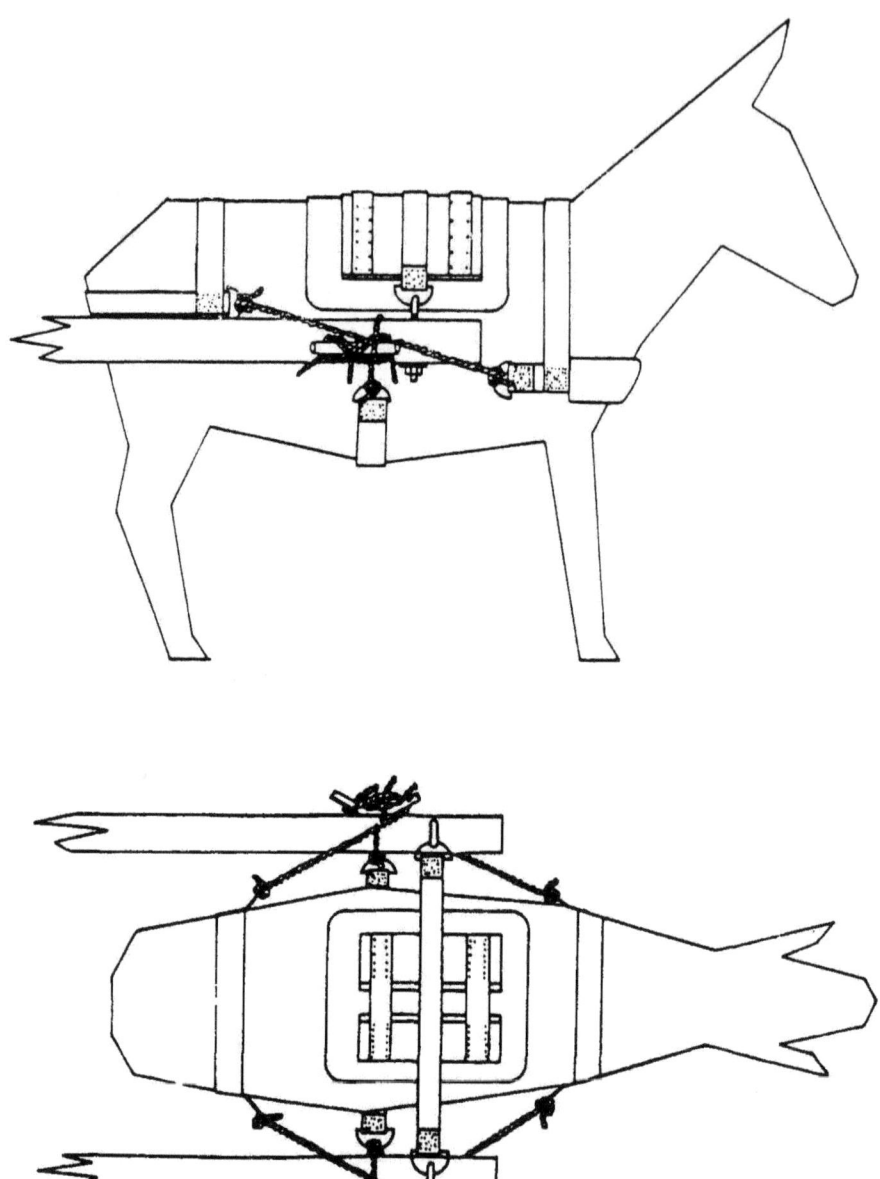

Figure 2.20 Breastband harness with adjustable breech, saddle and retaining straps.

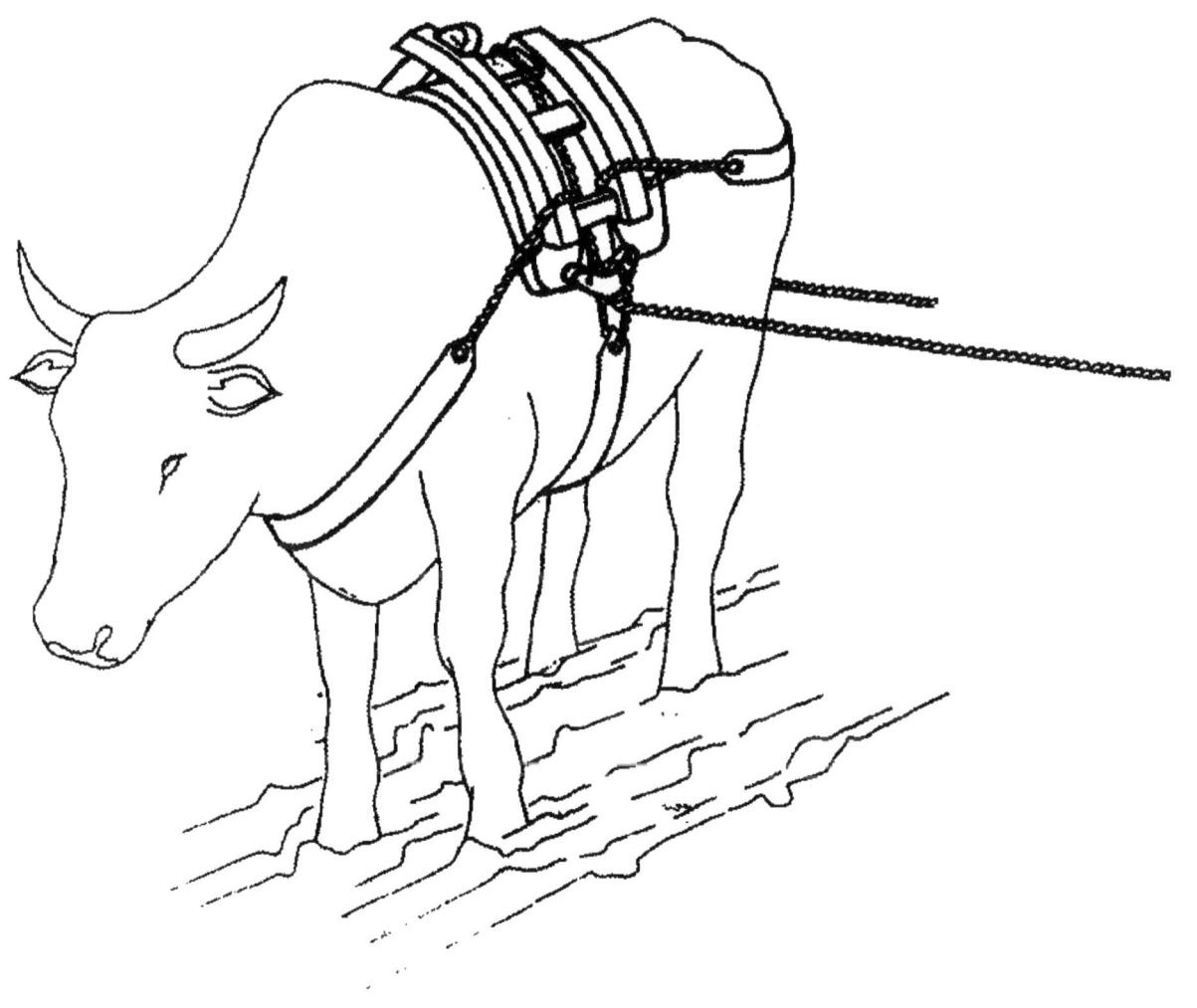

Figure 2.21 Saddle harness for bovine.

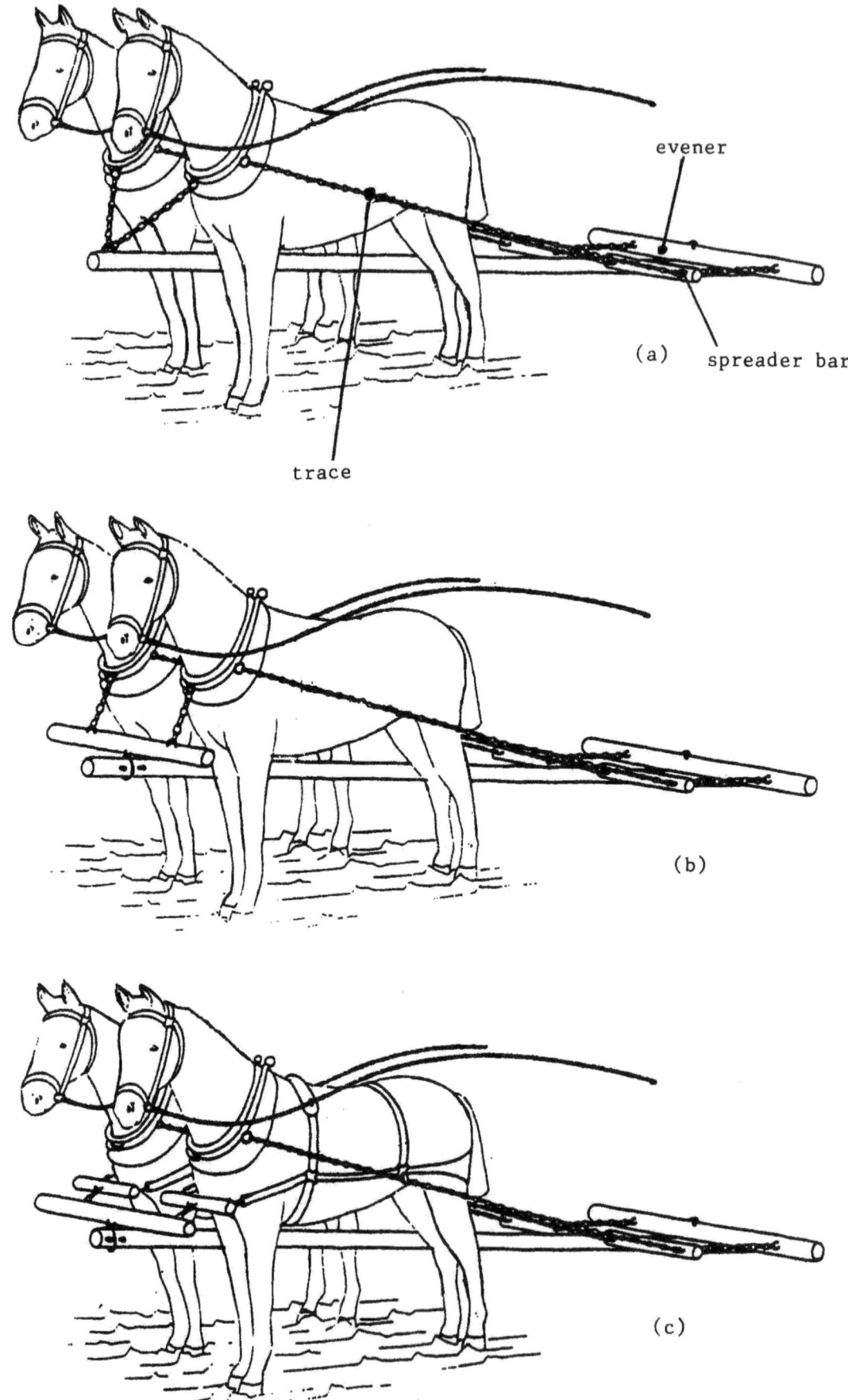

Figure 2.22 Three methods of hitching two animals with collar or breastband harnesses to a cart.

Figure 2.23 A single animal can support the load while others pull on traces: China.

Figure 2.24 A flat platform cart: The Sudan.

Figure 2.25   Two different carts with open-topped bodies, used in construction work: Botswana.

Figure 2.26   Bench seats for passengers fitted on top of the side walls of a general-purpose cart: the Lao People's Democratic Republic.

Figure 2.27 Purpose-built water cart: the Sudan.

Figure 2.28 Water bowser, constructed by fitting 200 litre drums to a standard cart: the Philippines.

Figure 2.29 Tipping cart used for construction work: Botswana.

Figure 2.30 Bottom dumping cart, used for construction work: China.
Source: Reference 5

Figure 2.31 Stake-sided cart: Bangladesh.

Figure 2.32 A solid wooden wheel, made of several rectangular pieces bolted together.

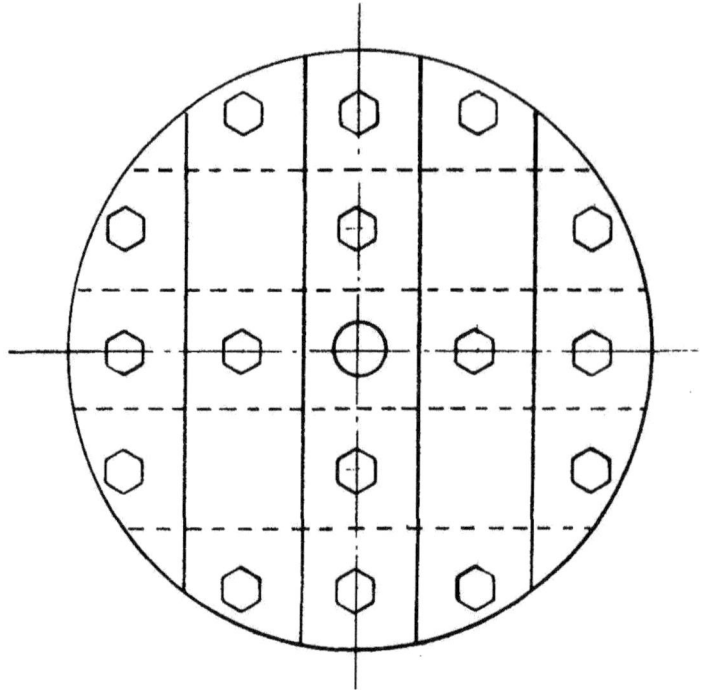

Figure 2.33 Spoked wooden wheel fitted with a steel tyre: India.

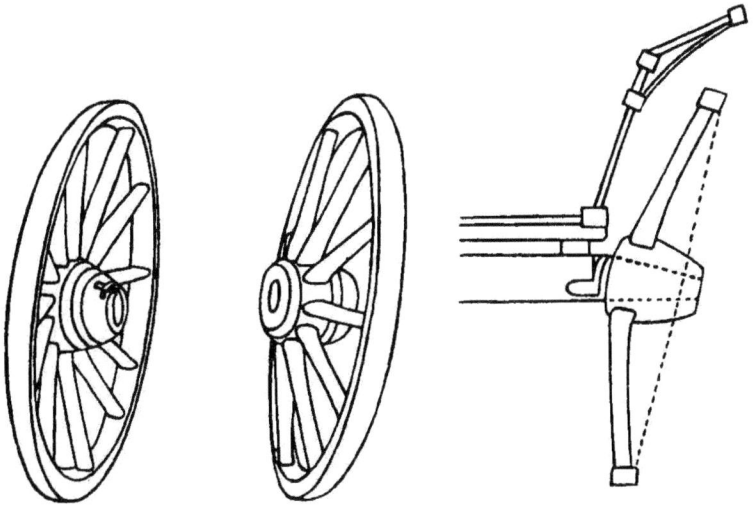

Figure 2.34 A dished wooden wheel.

Figure 2.35 A spoked steel wheel.

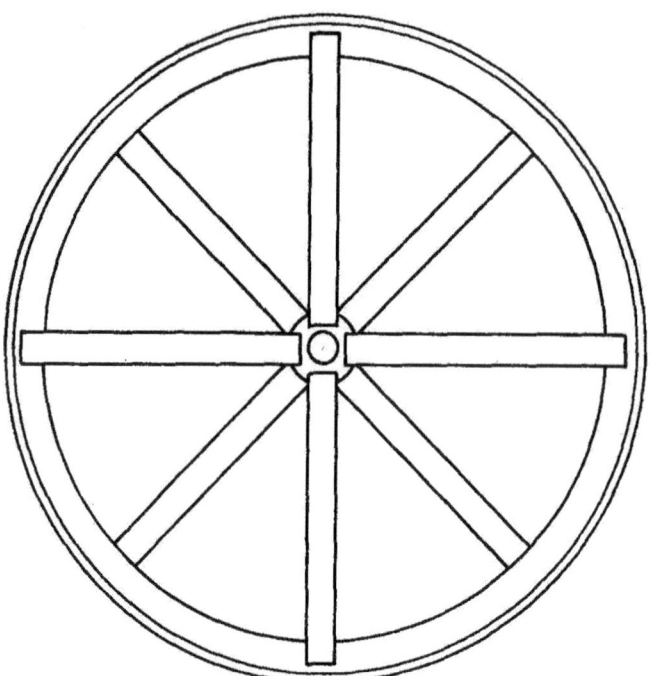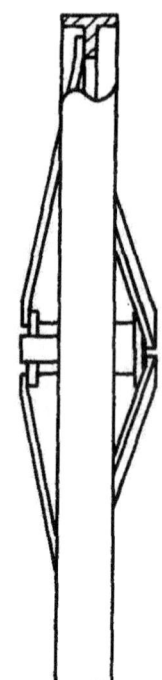

Figure 2.36   Steel wheel with 'T' section rim and flat spokes.

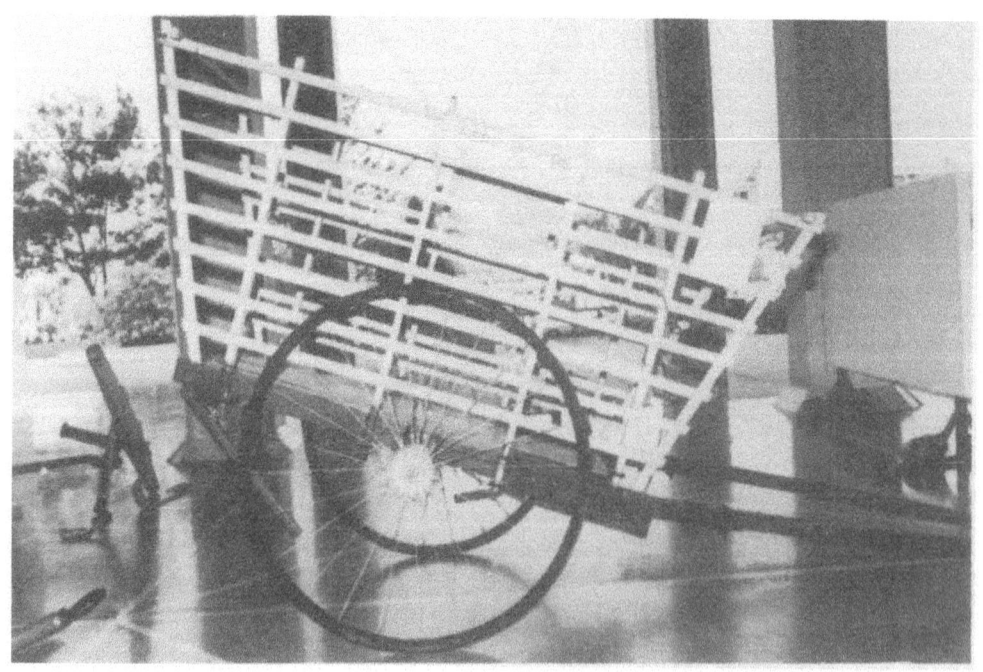

Figure 2.37   Tension-spoked steel wheel: Sri Lanka.
Source: Economic and Social Commission for Asia and the Pacific

Figures 2.38 and 2.39 Split-rim wheel to suit a pneumatic tyre: Ethiopia.

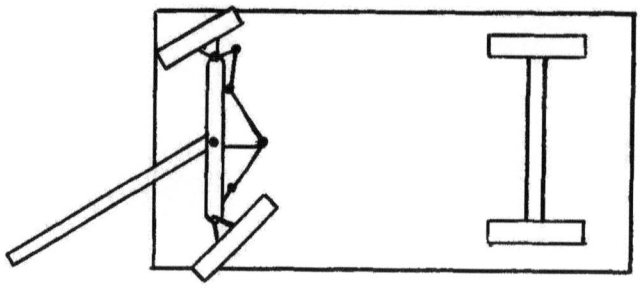

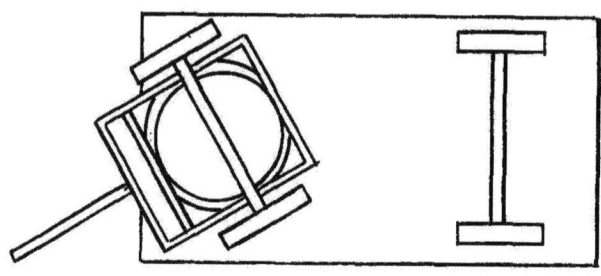

Figure 2.40 Axle pivot steering (top) and swivelling bolster steering (below) used on four-wheeled carts.

CHAPTER 3: GUIDELINES ON CART DESIGN

3.1 General Design Considerations

The previous chapter provides the basis for preparing an appropriate cart specification for a particular application. This specification provides the framework within which the designer must work to prepare a detailed design of the cart, and should ensure that the final product will be able to perform the required function and be manufactured and sold at an acceptable price. Working within the specification the designer must define in detail the design of the cart, taking into account the functional and aesthetic requirements, its intended selling price, and how it will be made. The technical details of cart design are discussed in the following sections of this chapter, but it is useful to consider some general design issues first.

3.1.1 Functional Requirements

Ease of operation will be an important functional feature for purchasers and users, especially if they are unfamiliar with carts. In rural areas, which will be remote from specialist repair services, it is desirable that the carts are reliable, and are simple to repair and maintain without specialised equipment or knowledge. In situations where cart operators have no technical skills, as will often be the case, the carts should be designed so that it is clear what any moveable and adjustable parts are for and how they work. Ideally only a few inexpensive and commonplace tools should be needed for repair, maintenance or adjustment, but if any special tools are required they should be supplied with the cart.

Where bolts are used it is preferred, if possible, to use only one standard size throughout to simplify maintenance. For example, three 10mm diameter bolts will have about the same strength as two 12mm bolts, and very little extra cost is incurred by specifying a size larger than the minimum necessary. Parts which will be removed frequently from the cart in use or for adjustment can be fixed to a length of chain attached to the cart to prevent loss.

3.1.2 Aesthetic Requirements

Aesthetic requirements are an important consideration but are often overlooked. Although the appearance of a cart may not affect how well it works, it can be crucial to its acceptance by the prospective user, or whether it will be purchased or not. Depending on local circumstances it may be necessary for the cart to look the same as existing traditional vehicles, or alternatively to have a more modern 'image'. In some societies elaborate decoration or simply a bright colour may be desirable, while in others a simple design will be considered elegant and attractive.

3.1.3 Cost Considerations

The purchase of a cart will be a substantial investment for a person of limited means. Purchase may be made easier by the availability of credit, but this consideration is secondary to ensuring that the cart is priced at the correct level for the local market. In some circumstances the need to bring the price down to a level that prospective purchasers can afford may be of such importance that it will override all other considerations such as efficiency, convenience and quality. The original specification and design of the cart will be the biggest factor in defining the price to the customer since this will determine the quantities and costs of the materials used. Designing the cart to simplify production helps to bring down costs, and the application of efficient production techniques will minimise the cost of manufacturing a particular design (see below). Finally, the approach adopted to marketing the carts will influence the sales price to the customer.

3.1.4 Manufacturing Considerations

As implied above, there is a close relationship between the design of a cart, its manufacture and the cost to the purchaser. While the requirements of the user are of prime importance, the designer must also take account of factors relevant to the manufacturer. The most important considerations are production cost; output and production rate; manufacturing facilities and skills; and materials and components. These factors are interrelated and cannot be considered in isolation. It is useful to define target requirements for each factor at the start of the design process and then work within those constraints to minimise cost and maximise quality and effectiveness.

<u>Production cost</u> is related to the cost of labour and materials. The cost of administering production includes the ordering and stocking of materials, and the capital and running costs of machinery, equipment and premises. Labour can be reduced by minimising the number and complexity of manual operations. Material cost is determined by the type and quantity of material used. As a general rule, the cost of material is directly related to its weight. Since many materials are supplied in standard lengths or sheet sizes, cost savings can be made by designing to minimise wastage. Administration and inventory costs will be kept down by minimising the number of different types and sizes of materials which have to be bought in.

The <u>predicted output and production rate</u> will be important in deciding the production processes to be used, and the extent to which it is worth investing in machinery and tooling to increase productivity.

The design must clearly be suited to the <u>manufacturing facilities and skills</u> which are available, and the choice of production process will affect cost. In general, except for large-scale manufacture, simple processes should be used which can be performed on general purpose machines. High productivity and the de-skilling of many tasks (which reduces labour costs), together with consistent good quality, can be achieved by using purpose-built production tooling such as welding fixtures and drilling jigs. Careful design of the components can make it considerably easier to construct and use such tooling.

The specification of <u>materials and components</u> is important not only in relation to cost and to production processes, but must also reflect what is easily available in the local market. In many developing countries it is not sufficient to specify simply from a supplier's list. Shortages frequently occur and the less popular sizes may be available only to special order. They are likely to be expensive and involve long delivery times. The best quality material may be allocated on a quota basis and hence difficult for a small-scale manufacturer to obtain. It is therefore essential to determine what is normally available in stock. All materials are described by a nominal size, and the actual size will vary, ideally within a specified tolerance. In many cases this tolerance will be large and, for example, materials sections which are nominally rectangular or round may not be so in practice. It may be necessary to determine actual tolerances by measuring samples of the material to be used, and the variation must be taken into account in the design. Certain sizes of components such as tyres and bearings may be substantially cheaper than other sizes because large quantities of them are used in particular industries. It is obviously sensible to specify the common, cheap sizes wherever possible. In general, specially imported materials should be avoided. However, if foreign exchange is available it may be sensible to import critical components which would be much more expensive, or could not be made, locally.

3.2 **Technical Details - Cart Structure**

This section and the next present technical information on various aspects of the detailed design of an animal-drawn cart. This section focuses on technical details related to the structure of the cart, while the next is concerned with the wheel assembly. They provide guidelines and examples of good practice that can be adapted by the designer to suit the circumstances in which the cart will be made and used. As the basis for discussion in these sections drawings are presented of eight cart designs, which illustrate their significant features.

3.2.1 **Major Dimensions**

The first stage in designing the cart is to define the major dimensions. In particular, the overall length and width, the length and width of the load platform, track width and wheelbase (for four-wheeled carts), loading height, ground clearance, centre of gravity and the wheel diameter and line of draught.

Several examples of carts are shown in Figures 3.1 - 3.8 showing the major dimensions. The <u>overall dimensions</u> of the cart are determined largely by the type and size of animal and the size of the load to be carried. The dimensions of the <u>platform</u> will constrain the size of the bodywork which can be fitted. Bulky loads such as grass or straw will require a much larger body than a dense load such as bricks. However in part this can be achieved by increasing the height of the body rather than the length and width of the platform. In general, the bodywork should not be made larger than necessary to limit the opportunity for overloading. If the cart is to be used frequently on routes with two distinct wheel tracks, the <u>track width</u> of the cart will have to be made to suit. If a standard full width axle is used, this will fix the track width. The track width will constrain the width of the frame, platform and bodywork unless they are positioned above the wheels, which is not desirable because of the high centre of gravity and loading height. <u>Wheelbase</u> is only relevant to four-wheeled carts.

For ease of operation the <u>loading height</u> should be low, especially if loading and unloading will be frequent, such as in construction work. However to achieve a very low loading height usually involves increasing the complexity of the structure of the cart. The loading height to a large extent determines the vertical position of the <u>centre of gravity (C of G)</u>. It is desirable to keep the C of G low for good stability, and, on a two-wheeled cart, to minimise the vertical loadings imposed on the animals in normal operation. The horizontal position of the C of G can be adjusted by altering the position of the load. On a two-wheeled cart the centre of the load area should be set slightly forward of the axle. With an evenly loaded cart this will minimise the vertical load on the animal(s) but still provide a slight downward load which helps it/them to maintain control.

Wheel diameter will usually be determined largely by the choice of type of wheel. However the <u>wheel diameter</u> and <u>line of draught</u> are directly related because the line of draught of a cart can be defined as passing through the point of contact of the harness with the animal(s) and the centre of the wheel. For minimum tractive effort the line of draught should be horizontal. This can only be achieved by using a wheel diameter twice the height of the animal's neck or shoulders, which is usually not practicable since it results in a very large wheel and a high load platform. The line of draught can be brought slightly closer to the horizontal by attaching the animal further away from the cart i.e. by increasing the length of the shafts or drawpole.

3.2.2 Frame Construction

The cart frame provides a strong structure to support the load and a convenient base for attaching the bodywork. The main aim of the designer is to fulfil these requirements whilst minimising the quantity of material used, in order to reduce both the deadweight of the cart and its cost. Careful specification of materials, and of design of the joints in the structure, will be of benefit in maximising the strength of the frame and simplifying its construction.

The <u>choice of material</u> will almost certainly be between wood and steel. There is little to choose between them as far as the performance of the cart is concerned, although it is possible to produce a somewhat lighter cart in steel than one of the same strength in wood. The manufacturing facilities and skills available may dictate which must be used, but otherwise the choice will be made on the basis of availability and cost.

If wood is used for the frame then the choice of species must be based on local conditions. Availability and cost of particular species are very dependent on local circumstances, but there are three general points that can be made:

    i) in many countries wood is becoming increasingly expensive. In order to keep costs down there will therefore be a tendency to specify poorer quality, but cheaper, wood. However the use of poor quality timber will shorten the life of the cart;

    ii) many of the high strength, good quality timbers available in tropical countries are high density hardwoods. Their use would result in a very heavy cart;

    iii) an important consideration is the 'workability' of the timber. It is important to select a wood which is easy to process by cutting, machining, planing etc., to produce the cart components.

Steel is usually available in a variety of cross sections. In general, large cross sections with thin walls offer a better strength-to-weight ratio for structural purposes than small, thick or solid sections. Rectangular or round tubes are excellent but are relatively expensive, and cause practical problems since, for example, it is difficult to bolt through them to attach bodywork or other fittings. The usual choice is between different sizes of angle, channel and 'I' sections of mild steel.

The structural design of the cart will be much the same whatever the load to be carried, but the specification of the materials will vary according to the weight to be carried, and to take account of the roughness of the routes on which the cart will be used. A simple rectangular frame of similar sized members is normally used, often with cross members to support the platform. This frame can be mounted directly on top of a full width axle or, more commonly, separated from it by spacers (see Figures 3.1 - 3.8 for examples). A full width dead axle is often an integral part of the frame contributing to the strength of the structure even though, for convenience, it may be bolted to the frame. If there is to be a space between the frame and the axle, the front and rear of the frame can be supported by longitudinal angled struts between the axle and the sides of the frame. In order to strengthen the structure against side loads, which are imposed on the cart when going across a slope or round a corner, further angled struts may be used between the ends of the axle and the centre of the frame.

The type and quality of the joints are critical to the strength of the structure as a whole. It is often necessary to make holes, or cut away some of the material, which creates areas of stress concentration. Careful design can minimise this effect. Strong wooden joints such as mortise and tenon and half lap joints are shown in Figures

3.9. These joints should be reinforced with screws and glue or bolts where possible. Coachbolts are conventionally used to form a strong bolted joint between two pieces of wood. However these are often expensive and Figure 3.10 shows a simple, low-cost substitute used to bolt two pieces of wood together. The bolt is formed from reinforcing bar, one end of which is hand forged to a mushroom shape. A thread is cut on the other end using a hand-operated die or, if available, a lathe. With a washer of suitable size placed under the mushroom head this provides a very effective bolt.

Joints in steel structures are usually made by welding. Bolted joints can be used but have to be considerably more complicated to achieve the same strength. There is much more variation in the design of joints for welding than when using wood because of the greater variation in the shape of the materials. Examples of good steel joints are shown in Figure 3.11. Many joints can be further strengthened by adding gussets. Good quality welding is essential to achieve maximum joint strength.

The structure of four-wheeled carts is rather more complex. When going over rough ground, all the wheels must remain in contact with the ground to avoid large torsional loads being imposed on the cart. To achieve this, either the cart must have suspension on all wheels, or the cart must be flexible against torsional loads. In addition, if swivelling-bolster steering is used, the front part of the cart must be very stiff. An example of a frame construction for swivelling bolster steering is shown in Figure 3.12 (this is the same cart as shown in Figure 3.8). A different type of construction suitable for axle pivot steering is shown in Figure 3.13.

3.2.3 Axles

A live axle has few advantages for use on a cart, and a dead axle is usually preferred. However the most common form of live axle is illustrated in Figure 3.14, and is also shown in Figure 3.3. The axle is made in two halves so that the wheels can turn at different speeds when cornering. The axles run in wooden bearings attached directly to the cart frame. The bearings for a live axle do not have to be made as accurately as for a dead axle, and the effect of wear is not as pronounced. The bearings are also better protected from road dirt and water.

A dead axle arrangement is considerably stronger than a live axle. The ideal arrangement is to make the two short 'stub' axles of solid round section steel firmly fixed to the ends of the central structural member of the frame. They should be carefully aligned, preferably in a fixture, so that their axes are co-linear and square to the frame. This will ensure that the wheels run straight. If they are slightly out of square the wheels will not run true and consequently the tractive effort required will be higher, the tyres will wear rapidly, and the road surface will be damaged unnecessarily. In practice it is often simpler to make a separate full width dead axle consisting of stub axles attached to each end of a structural member. This full width dead axle is then welded to the frame, or bolted to it with 'U' bolts or suitable brackets. An example is illustrated in Figure 3.15. This method is also used if the wheel/axle assembly is to be purchased from a specialist manufacturer. Recommended sizes of axles for different load capacities are shown in Table 3.1.

Another method of arranging a dead axle is for it to run through the wheel hub and be supported on both sides by the frame, as on a bicycle or as illustrated in Figure 2.2. This reduces the bending loads on the axle and thus allows a smaller cross section to be used, but it makes the frame wider and more complicated.

3.2.4 Suspension

The attachment of the axle to the cart structure will be more complex if suspension is specified. The simplest form of suspension is to use semi-elliptic leaf springs of the type used on some types of motor vehicle. Leaf springs are relatively inexpensive and simple to fit, and standard motor vehicle sizes are appropriate. Indeed it is often convenient to use the springs, mounting brackets etc. from scrap vehicles. A further advantage of leaf springs is that friction between the leaves provides some degree of damping effect. Leaf springs should be chosen to give full deflection at the maximum capacity of the cart.

A 'bump stop', such as a block of rubber, should be fitted between the spring and the cart frame in case of overloading. Sufficient clearance between the frame and bodywork and the wheel should be allowed so that the wheel can move freely over the full range of deflection allowed by the spring. The installation of the springs should be similar to that used on motor vehicles, with a single pivot at one end and a double pivot and link at the other, as shown in Figure 3.16. The axle is clamped to the centre of the leaf spring by means of U-bolts.

3.2.5 Harness and Hitching Arrangements

A good harness for pulling carts should have the following features (14, 15):

- does not hinder natural movements;
- permits reliable control;
- does not injure the animal (i.e. fits well, well padded, does not chafe);
- utilises the animal's strongest muscles;
- vertical loads can be supported easily (preferably on the back);
- some flexibility to minimise shock loads;
- simple to fit and remove;
- adjustable to fit the animal;
- permits braking (i.e. allows the animal to apply easily a backward force for braking and reversing);
- permits the line of draught to be as close to the horizontal as possible.

TABLE 3.1: RECOMMENDED AXLE SECTIONS FOR DIFFERENT LOAD CAPACITIES

Tyre Size	Maximum Gross Load per Axle (kg)	Minimum Recommended Axle Shaft Diameter (mm)
Light Duty		
4.00-19	740	32
5.00-19	915	40
Heavy Duty		
5.00-19	1220	50
6.00-19	1620	50
7.00-19	2540	50
7.50-10	2030	50
8.00-19	3050	56

Source: Indian Standard 4930-1968 Guide for axle assembly for animal-drawn vehicles.

The type of harness specified for a cart will usually be that which is already in use locally. Very few existing harnesses have the range of positive features defined above, though it is possible to modify existing harnesses to improve their effectivess. New designs of harness have been developed in recent years, each with its own advantages and disadvantages, and there may sometimes be opportunities to introduce these alternatives. The designer will normally have to specify the cart to suit existing harnesses, but there will be some choice about the type of hitching arrangement to use.

For a two-wheeled cart the shafts or drawpole used to hitch the animal(s) must be strong enough both to pull the cart and to transfer the vertical load. The vertical position of the ends of the shafts or drawpole should match the animal and its harness so that the cart body is horizontal. The shafts or drawpole form an important load bearing element of the structure of the cart, and in particular are subject to substantial bending loads. Their design should therefore be carefully integrated with the rest of the structure. One recommended method for a drawpole is to attach it directly to the axle (see Figure 3.7) which has the advantage of not putting additional loads on the frame (though the drawpole may also be clamped to the front of the frame). With this method the angle of the drawpole is determined by the wheel diameter, the size of the animal(s) and the length of the load platform. Unless a bent drawpole is used this can result in a fairly high load platform.

Alternatively a drawpole, or pair of shafts, can be positioned horizontally and form part of the frame structure (see Figures 3.1, 3.4 and 3.6). In this case, the height of the load platform is determined by the height of the hitching point on the animal(s).

A method which should be avoided is to simply attach the drawpole or shafts to the front of the frame or body. This system will impose very high bending loads on the joint, which will tend to fail unless the jointing arrangement is very carefully designed and integrated with the rest of the structure by some means.

A final requirement of shafts is that they should be as close together as possible for good control, but far enough apart to avoid hitting the animal while moving.

The shafts or drawpole of a four-wheeled cart must be attached directly to the steering mechanism. A hinge pivotting about a horizontal axis is required to allow the animal(s) to move up and down relative to the cart and transfer sideways movement directly to the wheels.

3.2.6 Bodywork

If the basic frame of the cart consists of a flat platform, a wide range of different types of bodywork can easily be attached. One simple method of constructing a body is to provide a vertical angle piece in each corner to which side frames can be bolted. Alternatively, one or more holes in each corner of the platform can be used to bolt on the bodywork. This may not be as strong as the former method, but it is simpler and it may be useful to be able to remove the bodywork and leave an uninterrupted flat platform.

The <u>choice of material</u> for the bodywork will depend on the same criteria as for the frame, although the manufacturing methods necessary are usually simpler. Sheet materials are often required, for which wood is often preferred to steel because it is lighter but still strong enough for this application. If the bodywork is to be subjected to frequent hard usage, such as in construction work, steel may be preferred for durability. The advantages of both materials can be combined by using steel angle or tube to make a framework which is clad with sheets or planks of wood. Bamboo is also worth considering.

Several design options for general purpose and special purpose carts are described and illustrated in the Figures in chapters 2 and 3. In preparing detailed designs for such bodywork it is important to make due allowance for misuse, such as loads being dropped or thrown onto the cart or placed on top of side frames. Any mechanisms such as tailgates or tipper catches should be robustly constructed and any removable component should be welded to short pieces of chain to prevent loss.

3.3 Technical Details – Wheel Assembly

3.3.1 Wheels

The choice of whether to use solid- or pneumatic-tyred wheels is made as part of the overall specification described earlier. The designer's choice will normally be between:

- wood- or steel-spoked design for solid-tyred wheels;
- split rim or standard motor vehicle design for pneumatic-tyred wheels.

A fundamental requirement of all wheels is that the rim should be exactly circular with its centre exactly in line with the axle centre, and that there should be no distortion of the rim. This makes the use of assembly jigs and fixtures essential during manufacture, except in the case of traditional wooden wheels produced by highly skilled craftsmen, who themselves use templates.

In designing solid spoked wheels, the diameter is of overriding importance. As the diameter of a wheel is increased its rolling resistance decreases, its cost increases and it becomes heavier relative to its strength. The magnitude of the shock loads imposed on the cart also decreases however, which enables a lighter construction to be used for the cart. The size of the wheel also constrains the size of the frame and bodywork and the amount of ground clearance. The width of the rim must also be chosen. A wide rim is stronger, causes less road damage, and usually has a lower rolling resistance than a narrow one, but it is also heavier and more expensive. The traditional method of constructing spoked wooden wheels is a complex skill which is only developed through years of experience. It is beyond the scope of this publication, but is described in detail in Reference 17. Figure 3.17 shows the structure of a typical wooden spoked wheel from Asia.

The construction of spoked steel wheels is less complicated with suitable equipment, and an example is shown in Figure 2.35. Welded construction is normally used. Ideally both rim and spokes should be made of material which has a good strength-to-weight ratio against bending loads, such as channel, 'T' or tubular sections. Flat rims and solid spokes are very poor in this respect, although they are commonly used. A flat section rim must be very thick, to prevent flattening between the spokes. There is considerable scope for the improvement of spoked steel wheel designs currently in use.

In practice there is likely to be only a limited choice about the size of wheels for pneumatic tyres. The wheel must suit the tyre, which will be chosen according to load capacity, availability and cost (see below for details of tyre specification). Conventional motor vehicle wheels can be purchased either new or second-hand, or a split-rim wheel can be fabicated. An example of the construction of a split-rim wheel is shown in Figure 3.18. The required rim diameter (dimension 'A' in Figure 3.18) is specified by the marking on the tyre, and is such that the rim will just fit inside the wire 'bead' on the inside edge of the tyre. The required rim width (dimension 'B' in Figure 3.18) is not marked on the tyre but, since there is a fairly wide tolerance allowable on rim width, it can be determined to a sufficient degree of accuracy by measuring the tyre. Table 3.2 gives the rim diameter and width dimensions for some common tyre sizes.

Because the tyre distributes the vertical load around the rim, the strength of the wheel can be considerably less than is required of an equivalent solid wheel. It is necessary however for the wheel to be able to withstand the high lateral forces applied to the rim edge when the tyre is inflated.

For dead axles the wheel assembly must include a hub into which the bearings are fitted. Wooden or steel spoked wheels will include the hub as an integral part of the wheel. Standard motor vehicle steel wheels do not include a hub, which has to be supplied as a separate item which attaches to the axle and onto which the wheel is bolted. It is possible to use standard motor vehicle or trailer hubs complete with rolling element bearings, or to make up a hub to take whatever type of bearing is specified. A split rim wheel can be made complete with hub, or can be designed, like a motor vehicle wheel, to bolt on to a hub. (Figures 3.18 and 3.20 illustrate a split rim wheel with integral hub. Figure 3.21 illustrates an assembly with a wheel bolted to a separate hub). Note that if a live axle is used the wheel attaches directly to the axle and does not require a hub.

TABLE 3.2 CRITICAL SPLIT RIM WHEEL DIMENSIONS TO SUIT STANDARD TYRE SIZES

Tyre Size	Rim Diameter (A) (mm)	Rim Width (B) (mm)
6.00-13	328	114
6.00-14	353	114
6.00-16	400	114
7.00-14	353	127
7.00-15	380	127
7.00-16	400	127

3.3.2 Tyres

Steel tyres can be fitted to wooden wheels in two ways.

A 'hoop' tyre is made in one piece from flat steel rolled into a ring and the ends welded or forged together. The tyre is then heated in a furnace, placed over the wheel, and cooled. The resulting contraction of the ring pulls the wheel together, adding considerably to its strength. A few nails may also be used to hold the rim in place should it become loose if the wheel dries out and shrinks. The diameter of the rim is critical to allow it to fit when hot and contract by a suitable amount when cooled. The process involves considerable skill and is described in detail in Reference 17.

Steel strip or 'strake' tyres are rather easier to fit, being short lengths of flat steel nailed to the rim so that the ends of the strip lie half way between the spoke ends. The strips can also be heated before fitting to help pull the wheel together on contraction, although this is not as effective as the 'hoop' method. An advantage of strake tyres is that they can easily be replaced individually as they wear out.

Rubber tyres are attached to steel rims or tyres usually by several large-headed bolts or screws, as shown in Figure 3.14. An alternative method is to use a channel section steel rim (which can be nailed or screwed to a wooden wheel) and hold the tyre in position by hammering over the two sides to clamp the tyre. Suitable rubber strip tyres can be cut from old truck tyres using a wet knife. Alternatively, suitable standard rubber sections may be available commercially in some places.

Pneumatic tyres can only be made economically in large quantities, and are often imported into developing countries. They are available in a wide range of sizes and specifications for use with motor vehicles to suit different speed and load requirements. Those suitable for use with animal carts are likely to be of the type used on large cars or light commercial and four-wheel drive vehicles. The specification chosen will depend on load capacity, availability and cost. The load capacity stated by the manufacturer is dependent on vehicle speed, typically up to 210km/hr for car tyres and up to 120km/hr for commercial vehicles. For use at 5km/hr, the load capacity is about 100% greater. Typical quoted load capacities are 350 to 500kg per tyre for car tyres, 500 to 1000kg for light commercial vehicle tyres (18). The size of the tyre is marked on it - the first figure is the width of the widest part of the tyre, expressed in inches or millimeters (6.00 inches may be expressed as 600). The second number, where used, is 100 times the ratio of the cross-sectional height to the width; the last figure is the rim diameter, usually a whole number of inches. It is always preferable to measure the tyre to be used, to be certain of its dimensions and those of a matching wheel.

It is desirable to standardise on tyre sizes to facilitate interchange-ability and repair. Scrap or factory-reject tyres should be quite adequate for use with carts as long as their structure is sound.

However their load capacity is likely to be rather less than the manufacturer's specification and they will be more susceptible to punctures. It is usually desirable to specify that pneumatic tyres be fitted with inner tubes, and this is essential if split rim wheels are used.

3.3.3 Bearings

Plain bearings

Plain bearings can be made of many different materials. For low friction and long life the bearing material should be hard and self-lubricating. The hole through, or bore, of the bearing should be only slightly larger than the axle, so that it will turn freely with a minimum of radial movement or 'play'. Excessive play will allow the wheel to rock from side to side which will push out lubricating grease and allow dirt to enter, and concentrate the load over a small area of the bearing, causing high friction and rapid wear.

Three types of plain bearing can be used, as shown in Figure 3.19. Plummer block bearings fit onto live axles and are bolted underneath the cart body. They can be made in one piece or split into two, as shown, for easier assembly. Bush bearings are usually pressed into the wheel hub. A one-piece bush bearing is simple to make, but uses a lot of material. A two-piece bearing requires less material, but is more difficult to make. All these bearings have a wide end face to provide a bearing surface for axial loads. Radial holes may be provided for additional lubrication. Care must be taken to ensure that these holes do not become dirt traps. Plain bearings must also be accurately drilled or turned, and fitted so that the wheel runs true about its centre and parallel to the direction of motion of the cart. Plummer block bearings, which are always used in pairs, must also be carefully aligned with each other.

The diameter of the bearing bore is normally determined by the size of axle required. The length of the bore should be two to four times its diameter, according to the hardness of the material. In general, the greater the bearing surface area, the less the rate of wear, but the larger the diameter, the greater the effect of friction. Washers must be fixed to the axle on either side of the bearing to transfer the axial loads to the end faces of the bearing. If possible, bearings should be fitted so that they are shielded from road dirt dropped by the wheels.

Plain bearings can be made from many different types of <u>wood</u>, in general the harder the better. Some woods are naturally greasy, and will require little additional lubrication. An indication of 'greasiness' is given if: the wood is easily polished; it does not react with acids; it is difficult to impregnate with preservatives; and glue does not stick to it easily. If the wood is not naturally greasy, it can be soaked in hot oil to improve its lubricating properties. This is done by boiling the wood in oil (e.g. old engine oil), until all the moisture is driven out of the wood and replaced by oil. The wood is now self-lubricating. This process also stabilises the wood and prevents it swelling or shrinking with climatic changes. Since the wood distorts during soaking the machining of the bore must be completed afterwards. The construction of oil-soaked wooden bearings is described in detail in Reference 19. Hardwoods can be used to make plummer block bearings as shown in Figure 3.14, or a one-piece bush can be made and pressed into a wooden or steel hub.

Cast iron can be used to make all three types of plain bearings by casting a suitable blank and then machining to suit the hub and axle. A radial projection may be provided to fit into a slot in the hub and so prevent the bush from turning relative to the hub. A longitudinal slot along the bore will help to distribute the lubricant.

Mild steel is commonly used to make one-piece bush bearings. These are very simple to make by cutting and turning a suitable size of tube, but steel is not a good bearing material, being neither particularly hard nor self-lubricating.

Other materials such as bronze or other hard alloys are widely used for plain bearings, but they can only be made economically in large numbers and are not well suited to low speed applications with minimal maintenance typical of use in animal carts. One material with good potential for use in animal carts, but which is little used at present, is nylon. It is easily machined to make one or two piece bush bearings from round bar. Nylon has an inherently low coefficient of friction. Friction and rate of wear will be reduced by lubrication, but this is not essential. Some grades of nylon are impregnated with lubricant to improve their performance. Although usually imported into developing countries, nylon is widely available and reasonably inexpensive.

Rolling element bearings

Ball and roller bearings are specified according to their radial load capacity when running and stationary, for a given life in terms of number of revolutions. In low speed applications it is the static load capacity which should be used. As two bearings are always used for each wheel, the load capacity of bearings to suit typical cart axles (40 to 50mm diameter) are generally well in excess of minimum requirements and so should give long trouble-free service. It should be noted however that where plummer block bearings are used with a live axle, the bearing nearest the wheel carries a much greater load than the inner one. Certain sizes of bearing may be relatively inexpensive if they are widely used in other industries. It may be worthwhile using a larger axle diameter and bearing size than is necessary to exploit the availability of a cheap bearing.

Many different types of rolling element bearings are available, but those most commonly used in animal-drawn carts are the ball and tapered roller types. They must always be carefully fitted according to the manufacturer's instructions to avoid damage during fitting, to locate the wheel properly, and to minimise wear in use. Grease is essential, although seals may be provided to reduce the need for repeated applications.

Ball bearings are cheaper and can be specified with integral seals which eliminate the need for subsequent greasing. Otherwise a suitable housing with a grease nipple will have to be provided. They will withstand axial loads up to 50% of the static radial load rating. A typical hub-mounted arrangement is shown in Figure 3.20. Ball bearings can also be purchased with a plummer block mounting for fitting to a live axle. In this case the self-aligning type should be used to accommodate distortion of the frame and axle under load.

Tapered roller bearings are standard fittings in motor vehicle wheels because they have a much greater load capacity for a given size than ball bearings and can withstand greater axial loads. They are also more expensive, although probably easier to obtain second-hand. They must be carefully fitted and adjusted with a lock nut to minimise play but prevent binding. A grease nipple must be provided in the housing unless it is perfectly sealed. The better the seal the less often will lubrication be required. A typical arrangement is shown in Figure 3.21. Tapered roller bearings cannot be used with plummer block housings.

3.3.4 Brakes

Three types of brake are suitable for use in animal-drawn carts: rim brakes, drum brakes and band brakes, as shown in Figure 3.22. Whichever type is used, the strength of the axle must allow for the additional loads imposed on it when the brake is used.

The simplest form of brake acts on the outside surface of the tyre, and may simply consist of a moveable bar of steel or wood running across the underside of the cart. For better friction and reduced wear however, brake shoes with a friction lining are preferred. Wood, leather or rubber is adequate, or motor vehicle-type linings can be used. A typical arrangement is shown in Figure 3.23. The shoes are pulled into contact with the wheels by a linkage attached to the bar and operated by a lever near the driver. The linkage should include an equalising mechanism so that the same braking force is applied to both wheels. A ratchet on the operating lever will allow the brakes to be locked on for parking. If split-rim wheels with a wide rim are used, a similar arrangement can be used to apply the brake shoes to the inside of the rim, which will give better protection from dirt and water. Another very simple arrangement, used on some traditional Indian carts, simply uses a rope to apply the brake bar, as shown in Figure 3.24.

If a conventional motor vehicle wheel and hub is used, the integral drum brake mechanism can be used. A sleeved cable linkage is best, but a steel rod mechanism can be used instead. An equaliser is again required. This type of brake is considerably more complicated and difficult to maintain than the others. It may however be the cheapest method if the parts are obtained second-hand as part of the wheel/axle assembly.

If a live axle is used it may be better to use band brakes, which consist of a drum fixed to each of the half axles. A steel band with a friction lining is pulled against the outside of the drum to provide the braking force. The operating mechanism also requires an equaliser, but otherwise it is relatively simple because the brake drums can be fitted close together, near the centre of the cart.

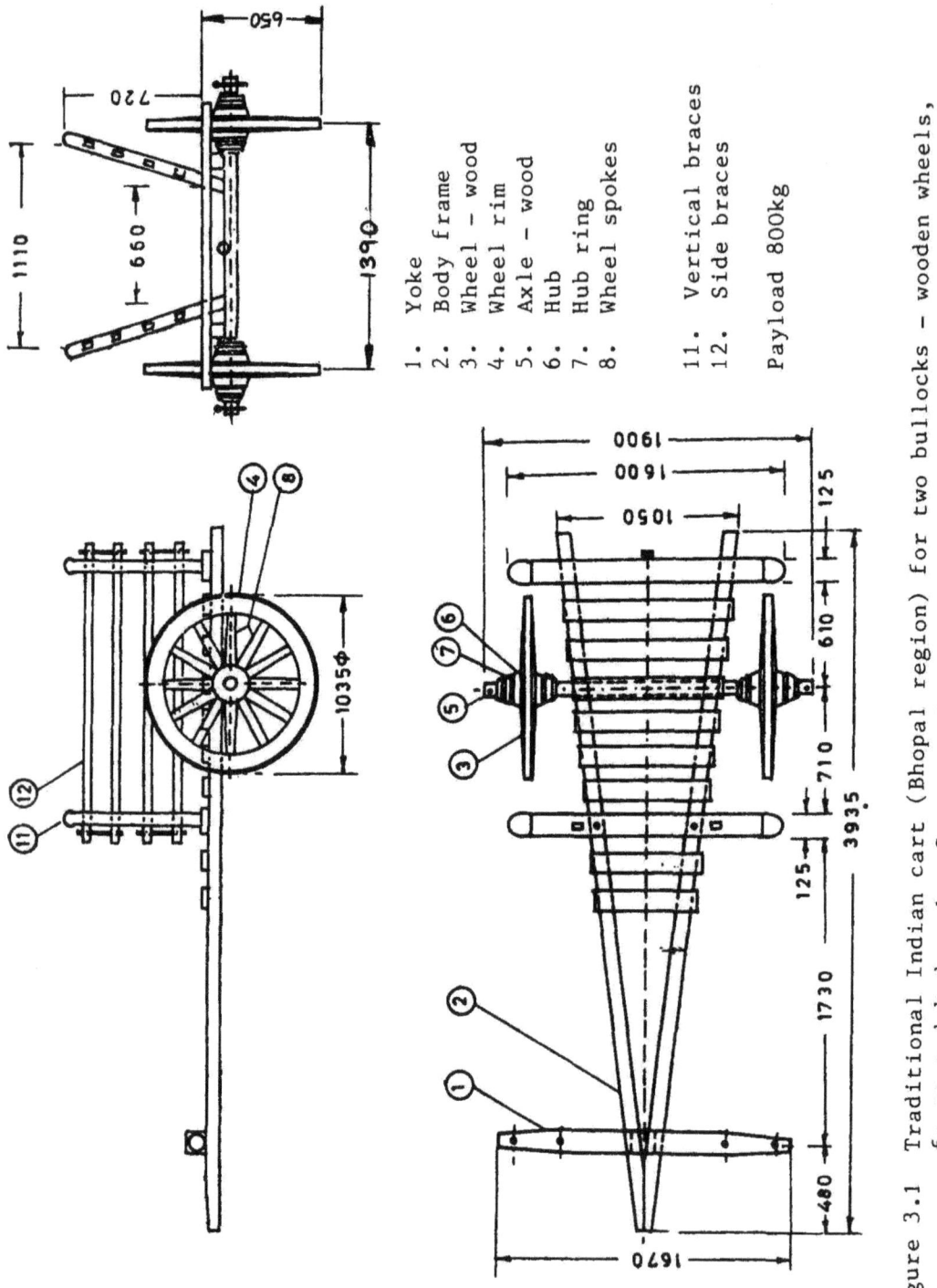

Figure 3.1 Traditional Indian cart (Bhopal region) for two bullocks - wooden wheels, frame and bodywork. Source: Central Institute of Agricultural Engineering, Bhopal.

1. Yoke
2. Body frame
3. Wheel - wood
4. Wheel rim
5. Axle - wood
6. Hub
7. Hub ring
8. Wheel spokes
11. Vertical braces
12. Side braces

Payload 800kg

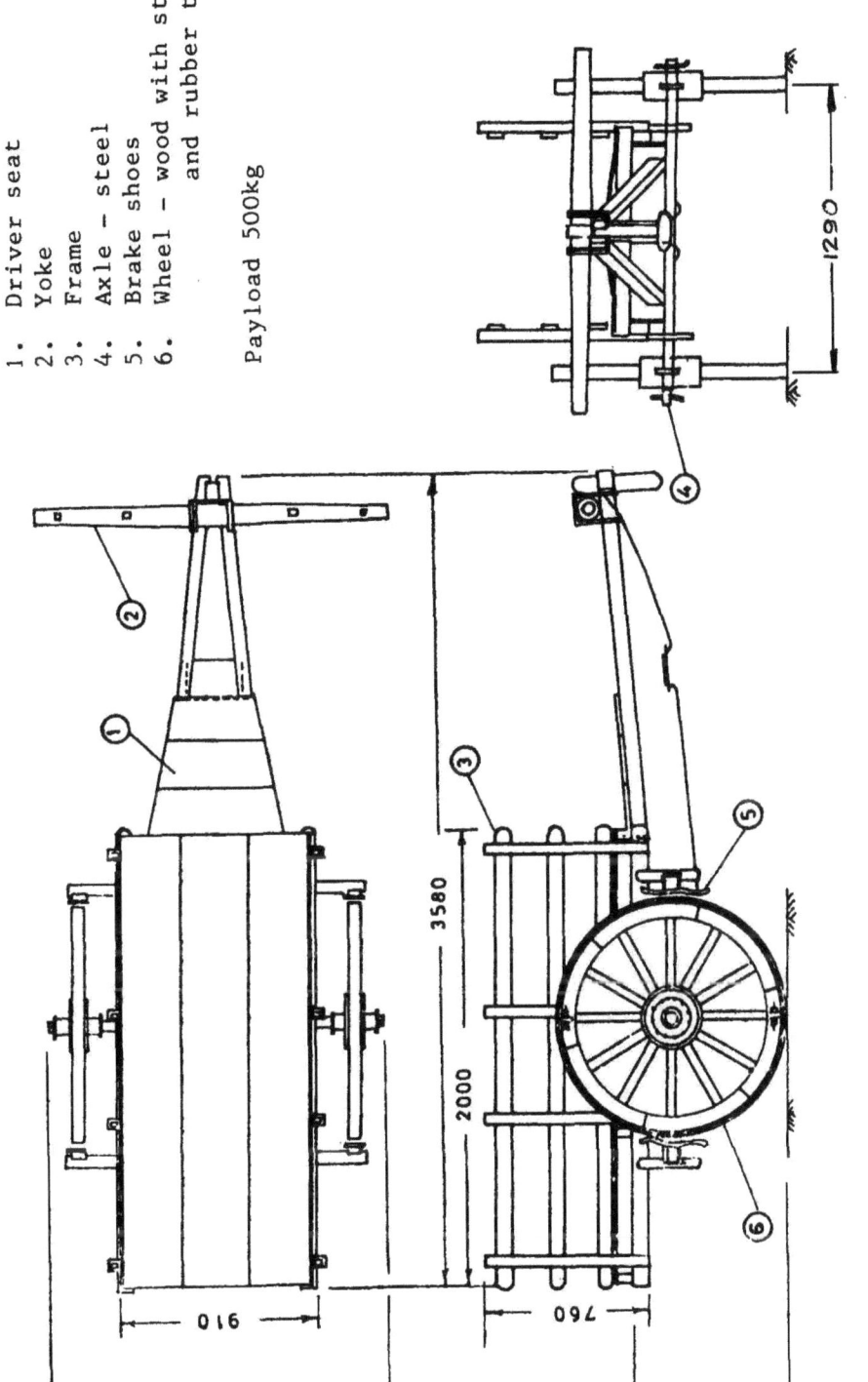

Figure 3.2 Improved version of traditional Indian cart- steel axle, bamboo and wood frame. Source: Central Institute of Agricultural Engineering, Bhopal.

1. Driver seat
2. Yoke
3. Frame
4. Axle – steel
5. Brake shoes
6. Wheel – wood with steel and rubber tyre

Payload 500kg

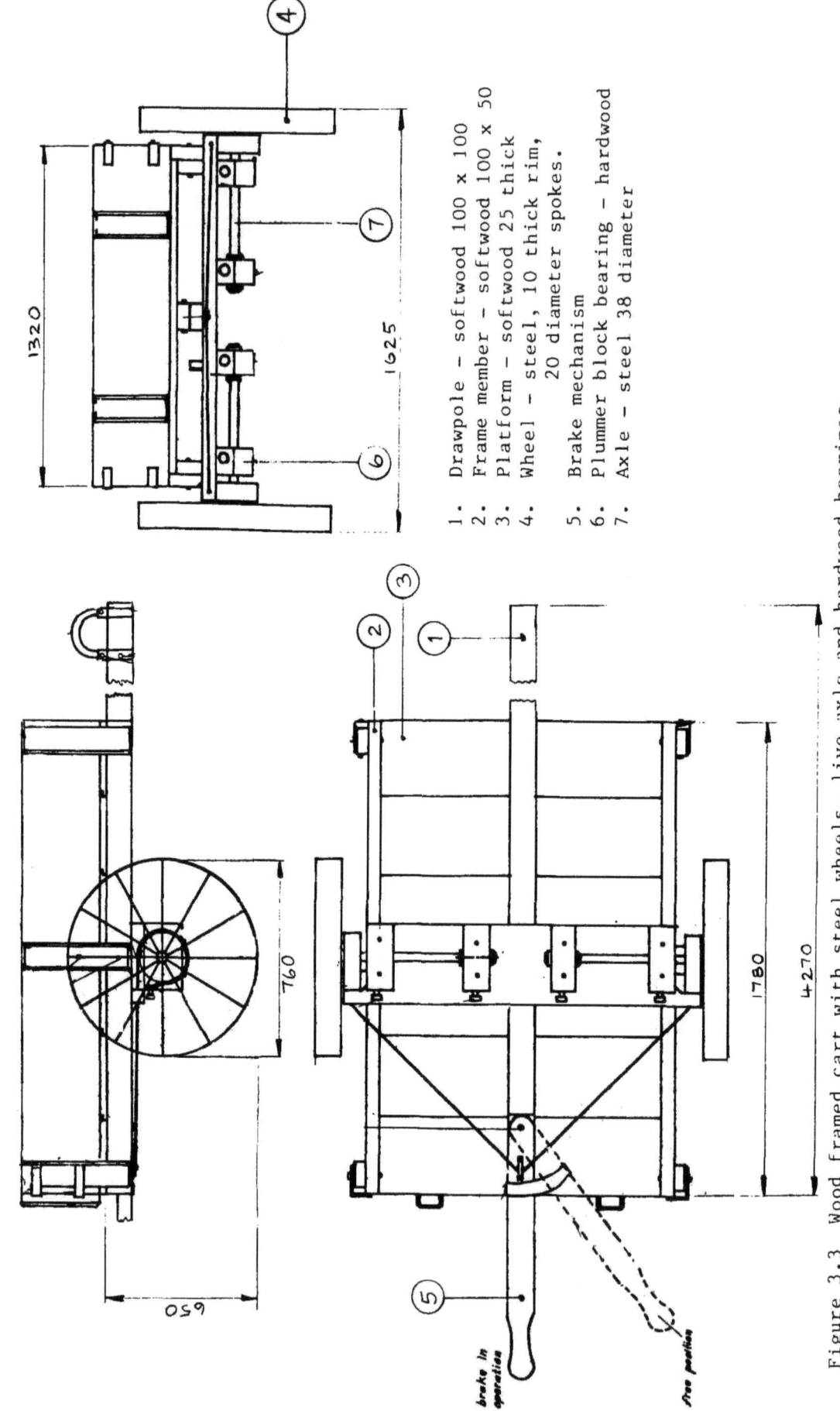

Figure 3.3 Wood framed cart with steel wheels, live axle and hardwood bearings.
Source: TAMTU, United Republic of Tanzania.

1. Drawpole – softwood 100 x 100
2. Frame member – softwood 100 x 50
3. Platform – softwood 25 thick
4. Wheel – steel, 10 thick rim, 20 diameter spokes.
5. Brake mechanism
6. Plummer block bearing – hardwood
7. Axle – steel 38 diameter

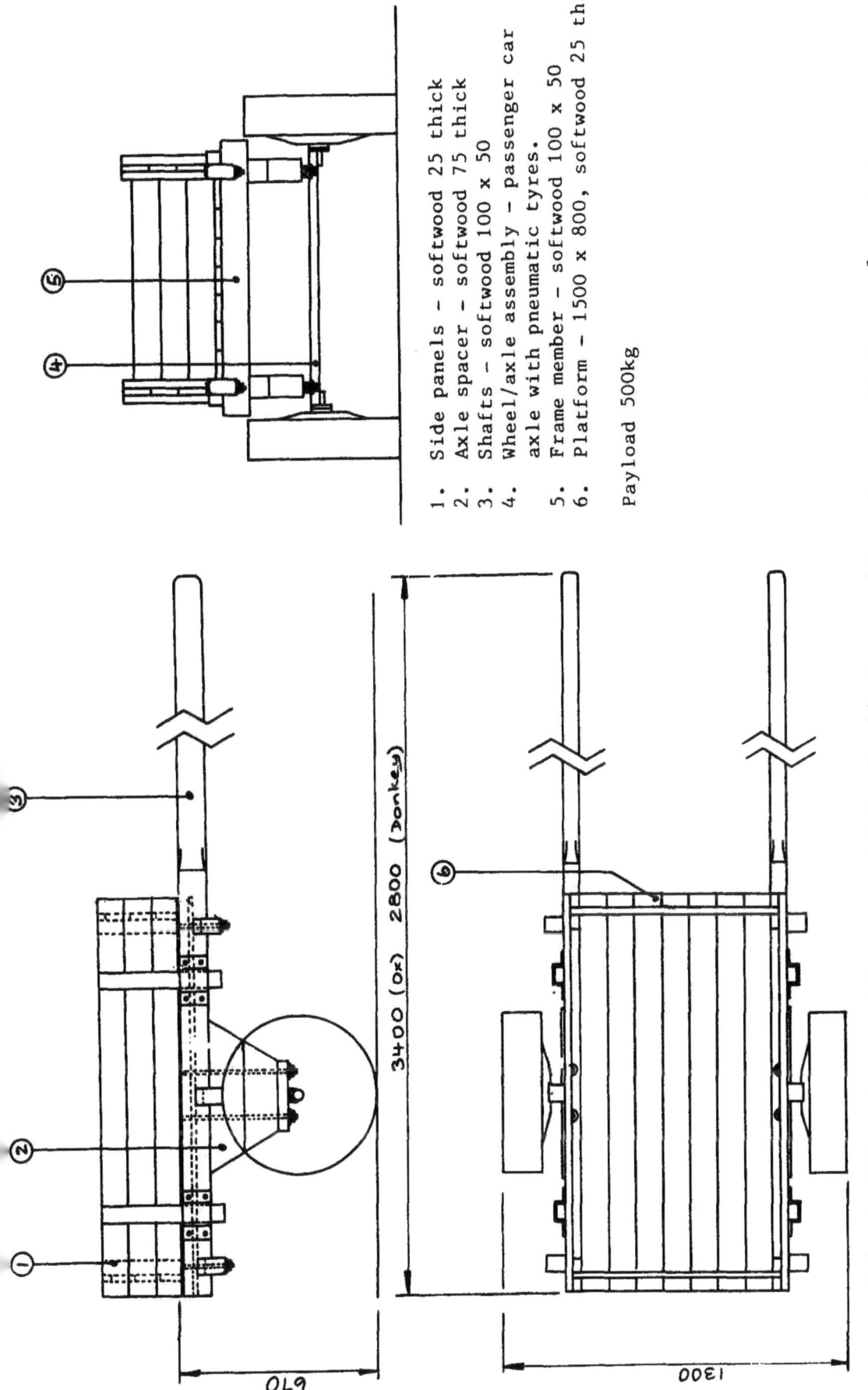

Figure 3.4 Wood framed cart with motor vehicle wheel/axle assembly and pneumatic tyres, for one ox or donkey; the Sudan.

1. Side panels - softwood 25 thick
2. Axle spacer - softwood 75 thick
3. Shafts - softwood 100 x 50
4. Wheel/axle assembly - passenger car axle with pneumatic tyres.
5. Frame member - softwood 100 x 50
6. Platform - 1500 x 800, softwood 25 th.

Payload 500kg

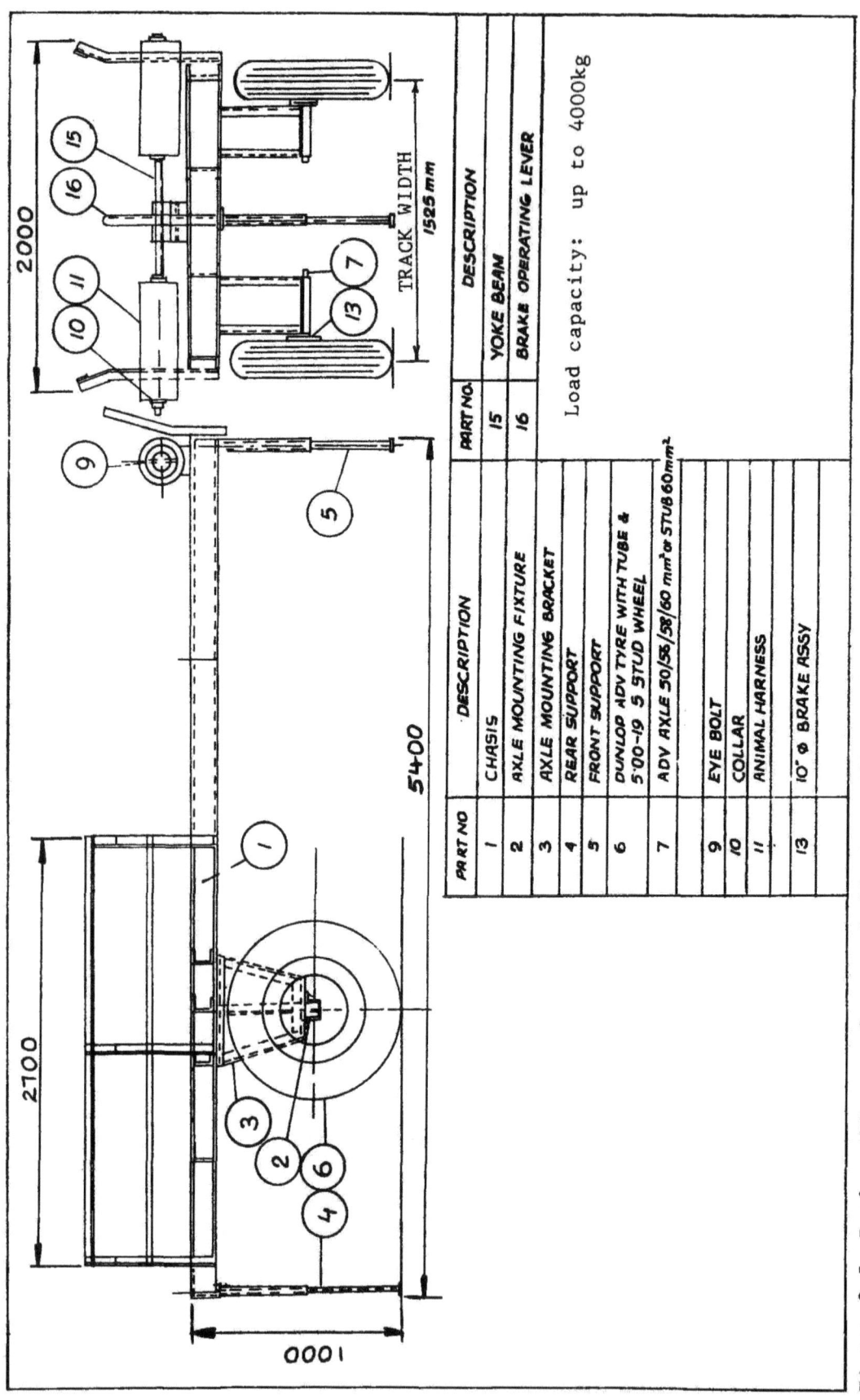

Figure 3.5 Dunlop ADV cart for two bullocks. All-steel construction, pneumatic tyres: India.

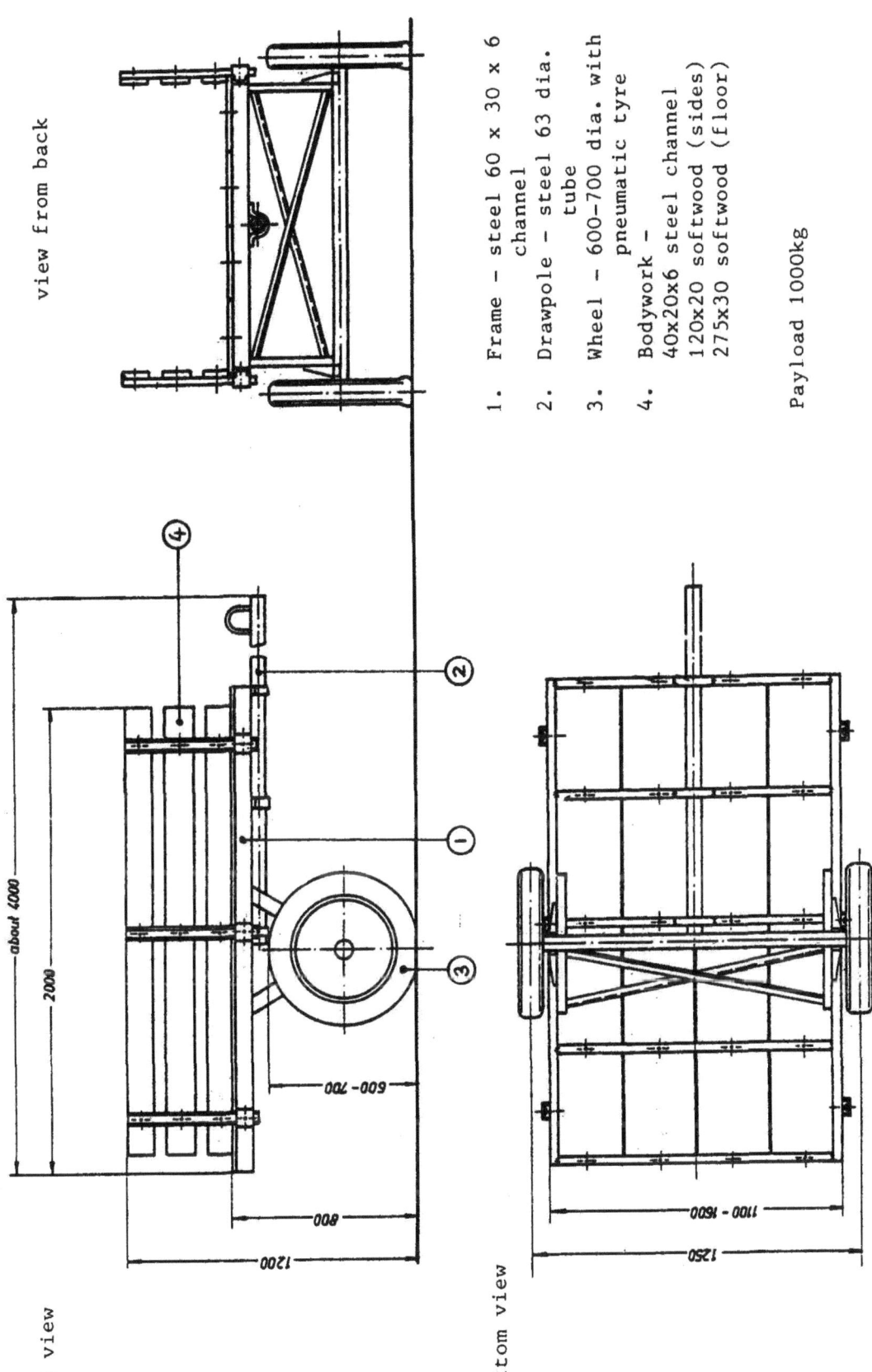

Figure 3.6 Steel framed cart with fabricated wheel/axle assembly and pneumatic tyres for two bullocks. Source: SISMAR, Senegal (reconstructed by GTZ).

1. Frame - steel 60 x 30 x 6 channel
2. Drawpole - steel 63 dia. tube
3. Wheel - 600-700 dia. with pneumatic tyre
4. Bodywork - 40x20x6 steel channel
   120x20 softwood (sides)
   275x30 softwood (floor)

Payload 1000kg

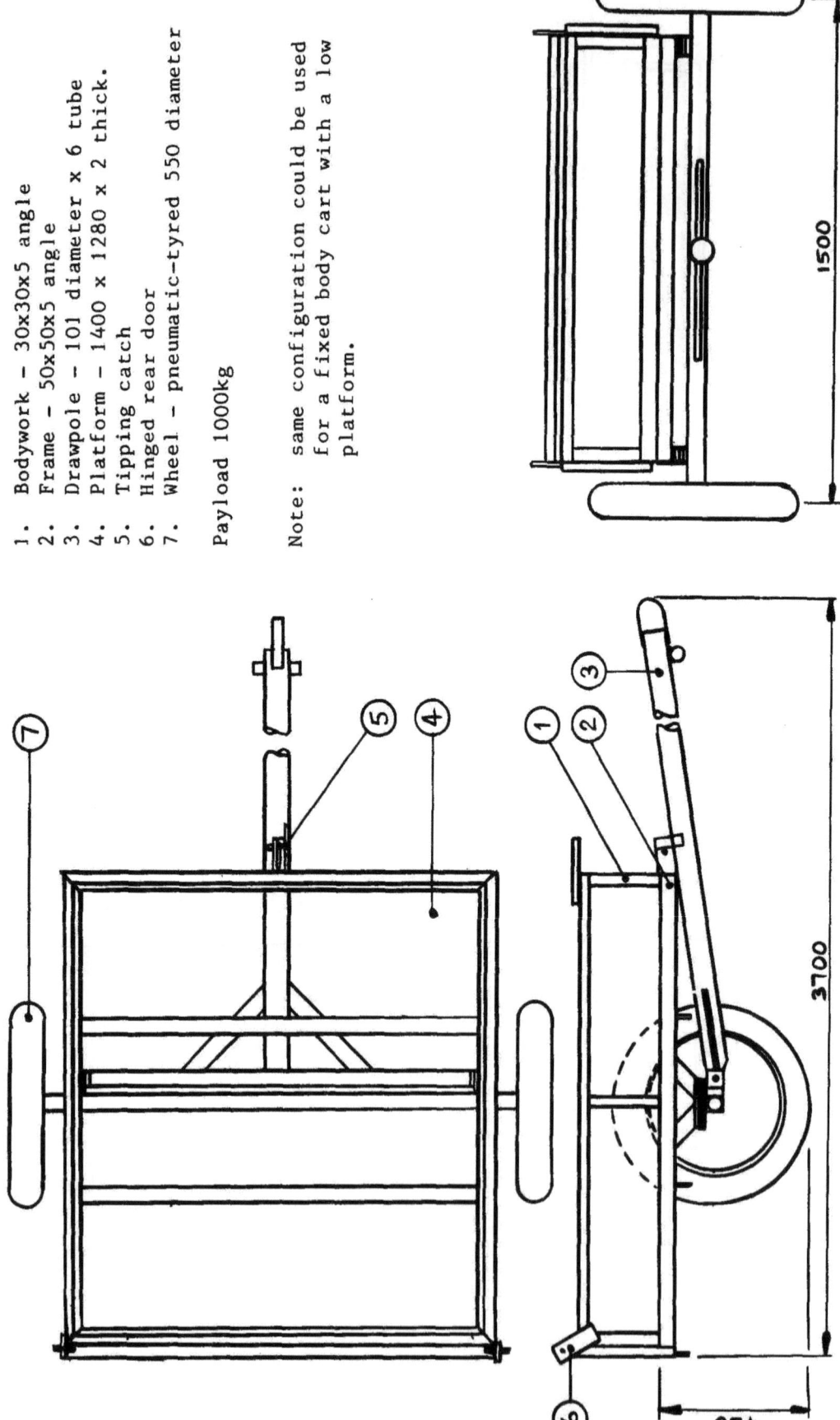

1. Bodywork – 30x30x5 angle
2. Frame – 50x50x5 angle
3. Drawpole – 101 diameter x 6 tube
4. Platform – 1400 x 1280 x 2 thick.
5. Tipping catch
6. Hinged rear door
7. Wheel – pneumatic-tyred 550 diameter

Payload 1000kg

Note: same configuration could be used for a fixed body cart with a low platform.

Figure 3.7 All-steel tipping cart with pneumatic tyres, for two donkeys. Source: International Labour Organisation, Botswana.

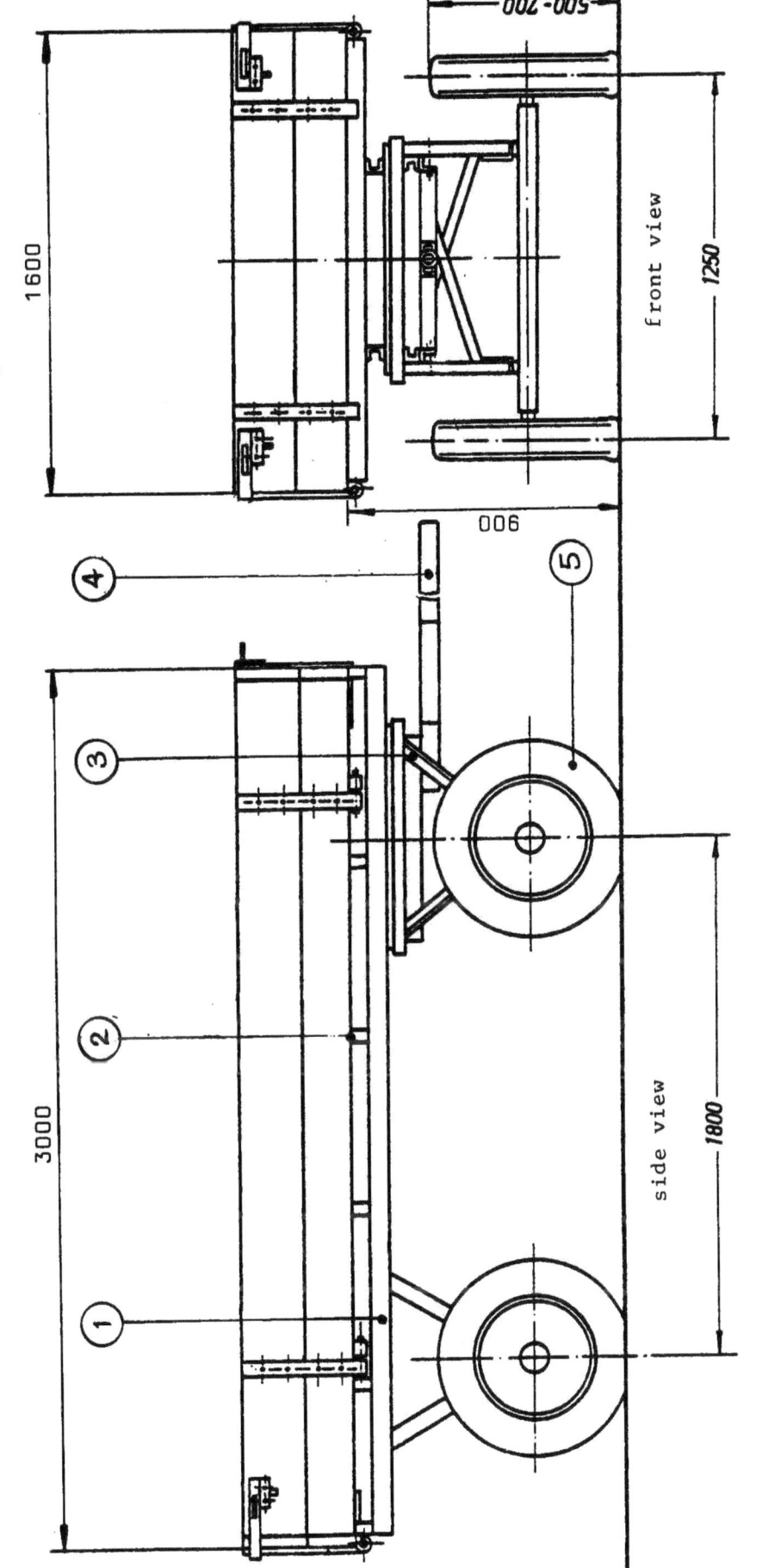

Figure 3.8 Four-wheeled cart, steel framed, wooden body, with pneumatic tyres, for two oxen.
Source: GTZ.

1. Frame – steel, 80x45x8 channel (longitudinal members) 60x30x6 channel (cross members)
2. Bodywork – softwood, 40x60 (base), 200x25 (sides)
3. Front axle assembly – steel channel 60x30x6
4. Drawpole – steel, 63 diameter tube
5. Wheels – pneumatic-tyred 500-700 dia.

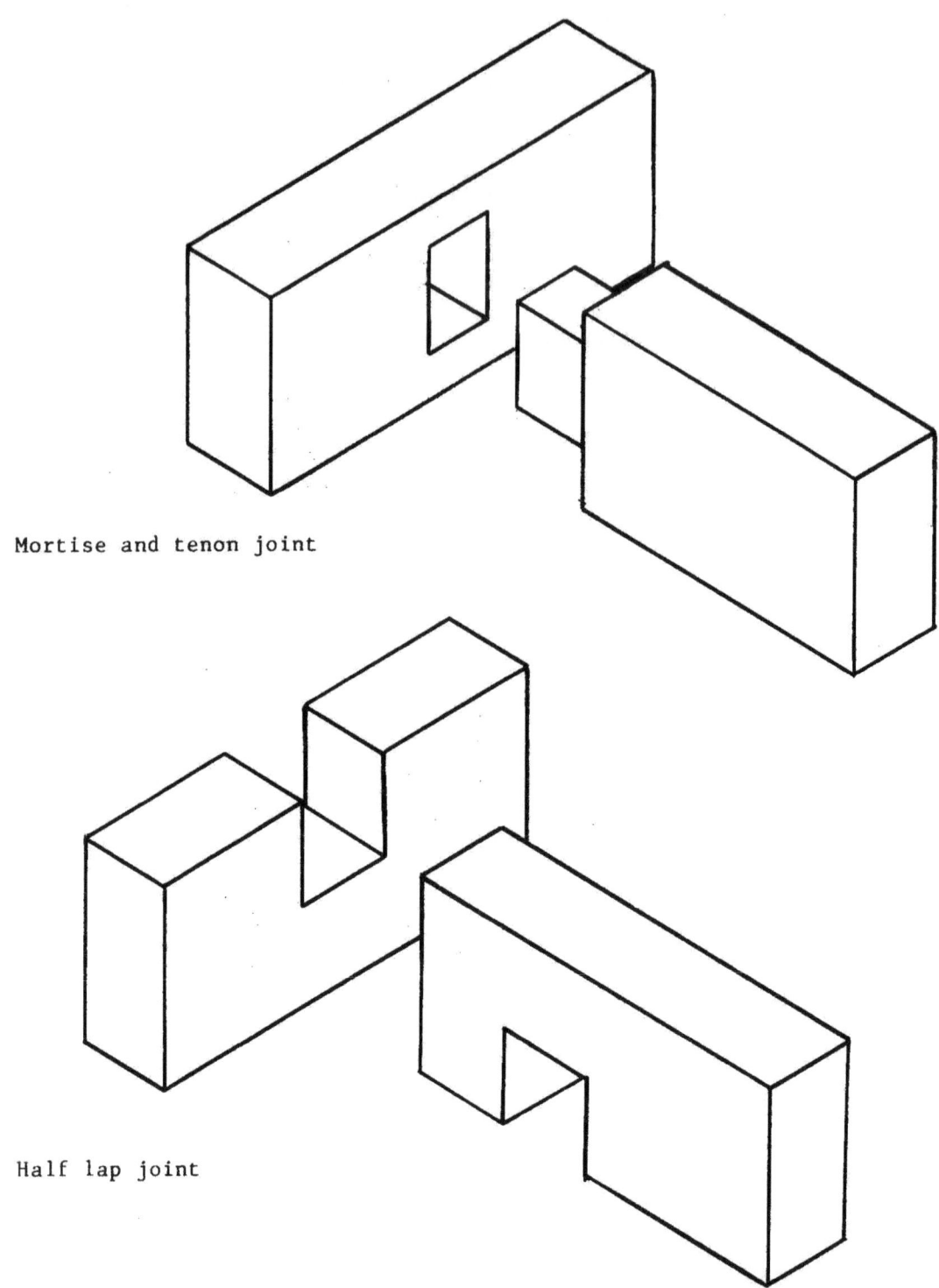

Figure 3.9 Strong wooden joints.

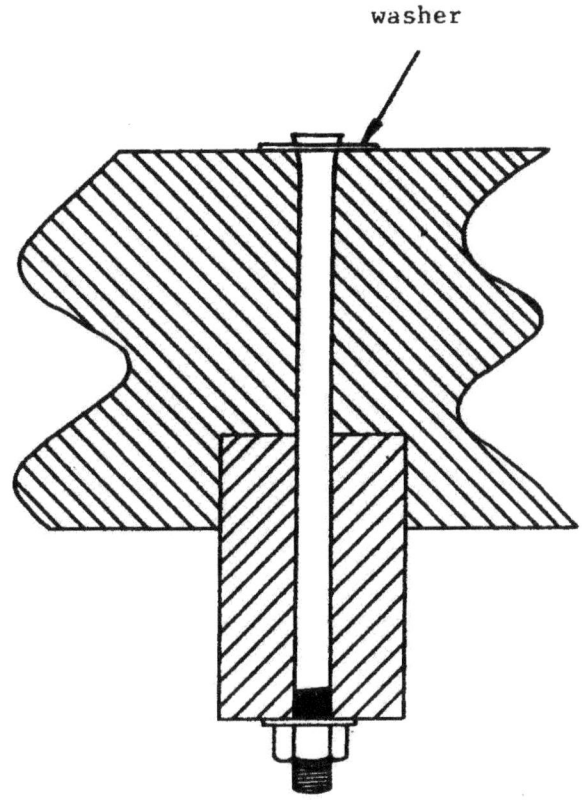

Figure 3.10 Low-cost coach bolt made from reinforcing bar.

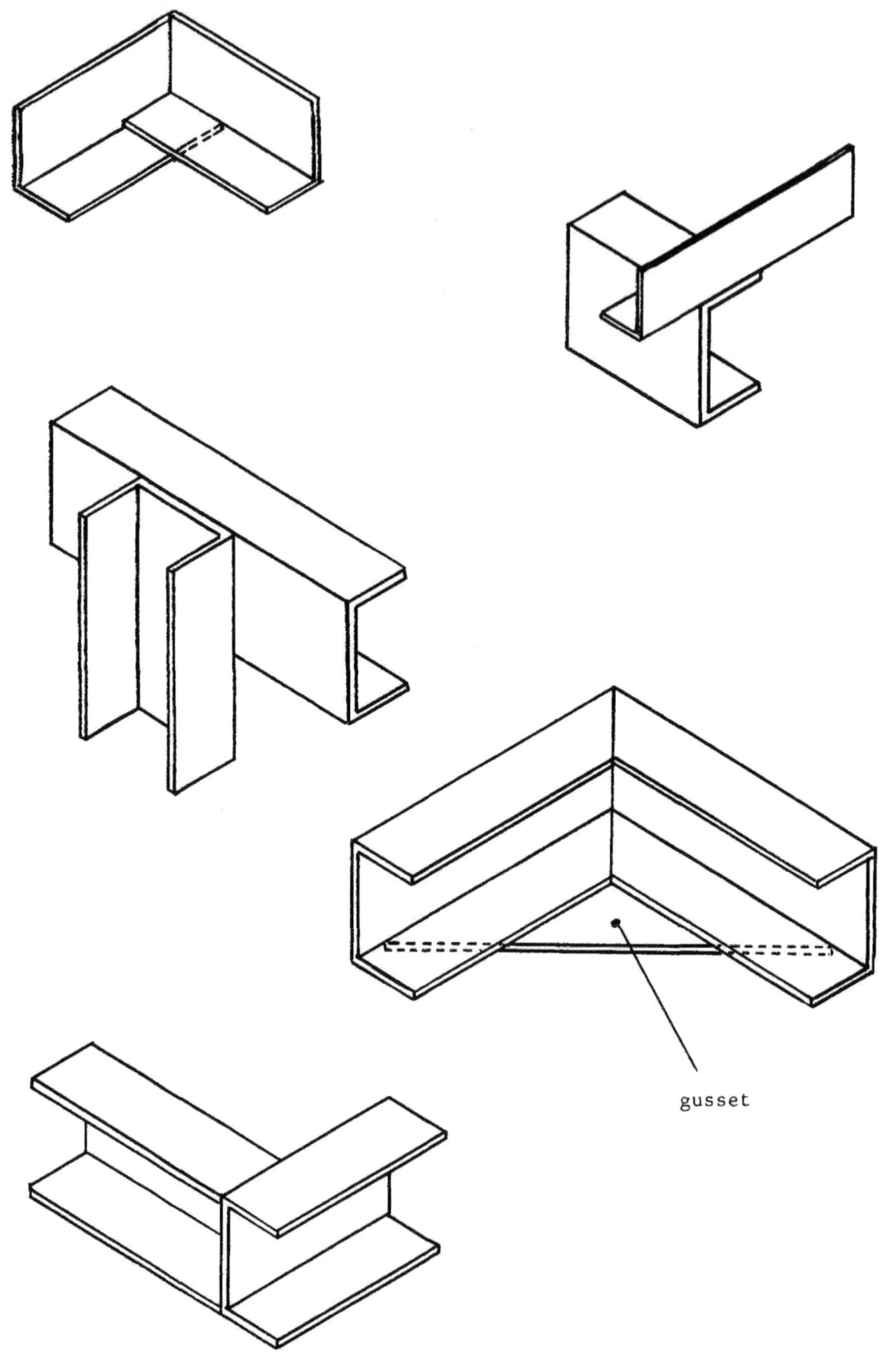

Figure 3.11 Strong steel joints.

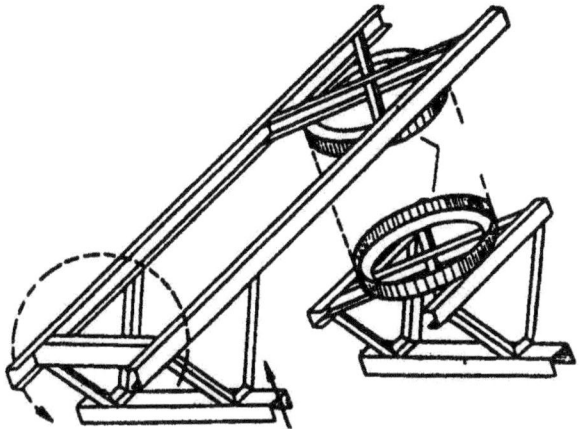

Figure 3.12 Frame construction for swivelling bolster steering, with flexible rear part and stiff front part.
Source: GTZ.

Figure 3.13 Frame construction with axle pivot steering.
Source: TAMTU, United Republic of Tanzania.

Figure 3.14 A live axle arrangement with wooden bearings: United Republic of Tanzania.

Figure 3.15 A wheel/axle assembly with stub axles, bolted to a wooden cart: United Republic of Tanzania.

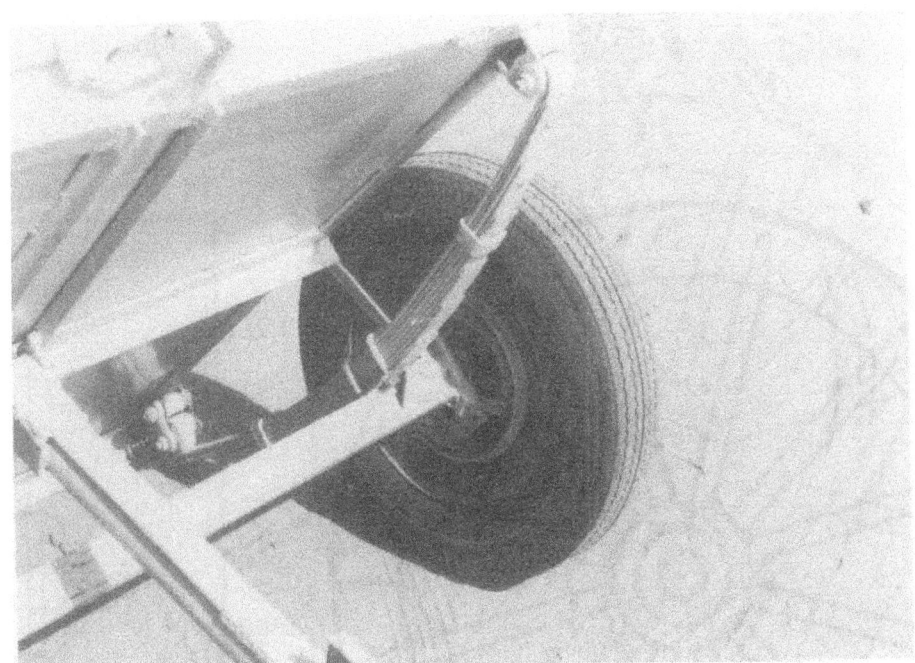

Figure 3.16 Leaf spring fitted to a tipping cart: Botswana.

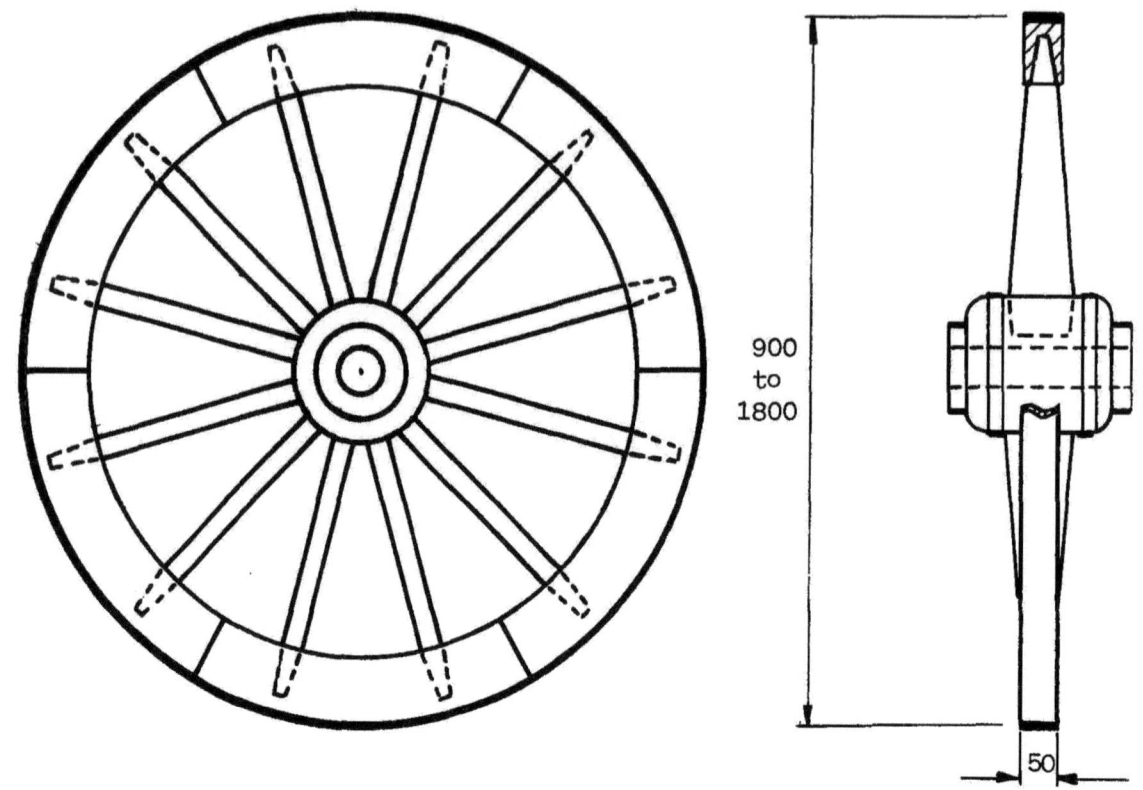

Figure 3.17 Traditional Asian wooden spoked wheel.

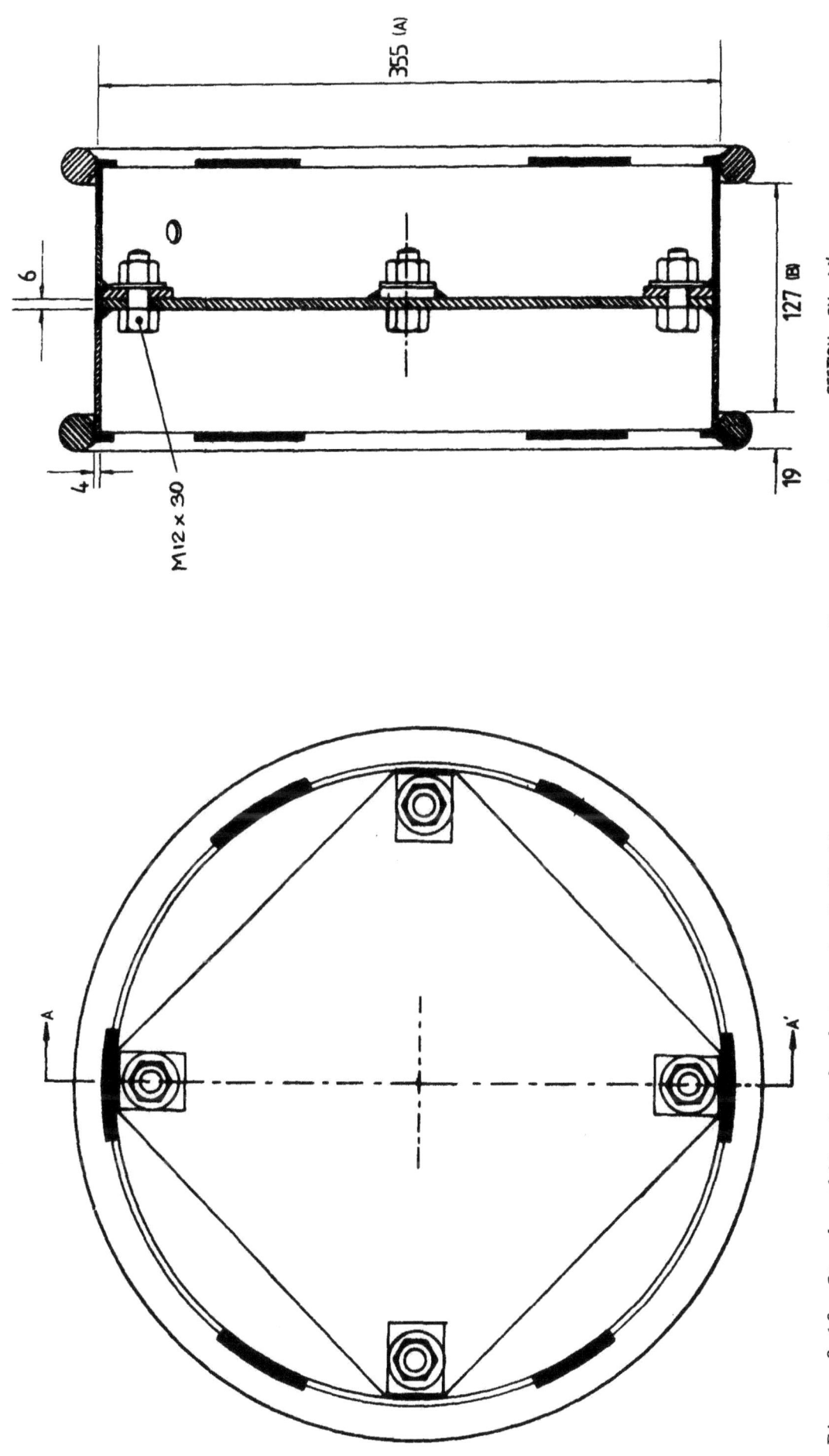

Figure 3.18 Steel split-rim wheel to suit 7.00-14 pneumatic tyre (hub omitted).

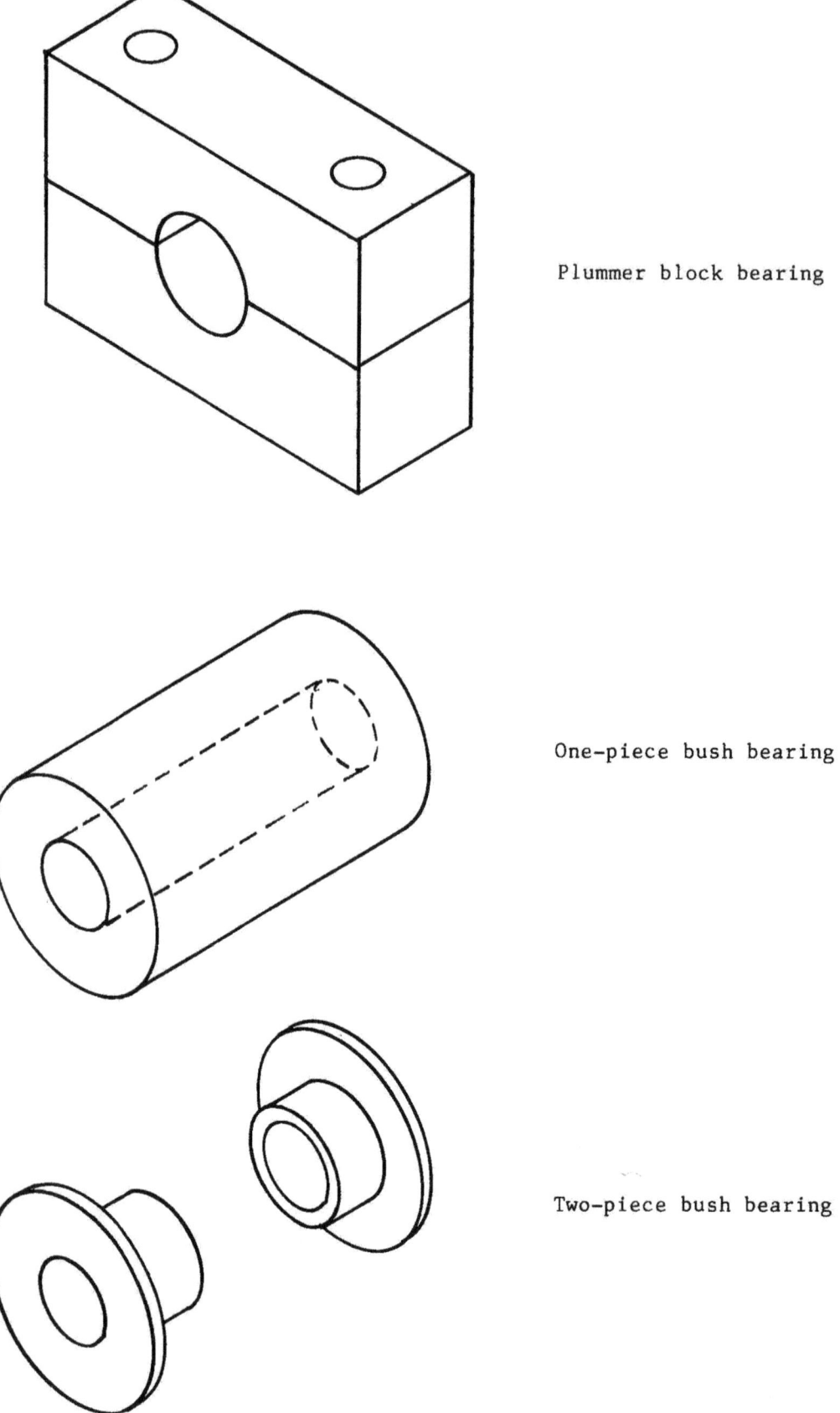

Figure 3.19 Three types of plain bearing.

INNER WASHER WELDED TO AXLE

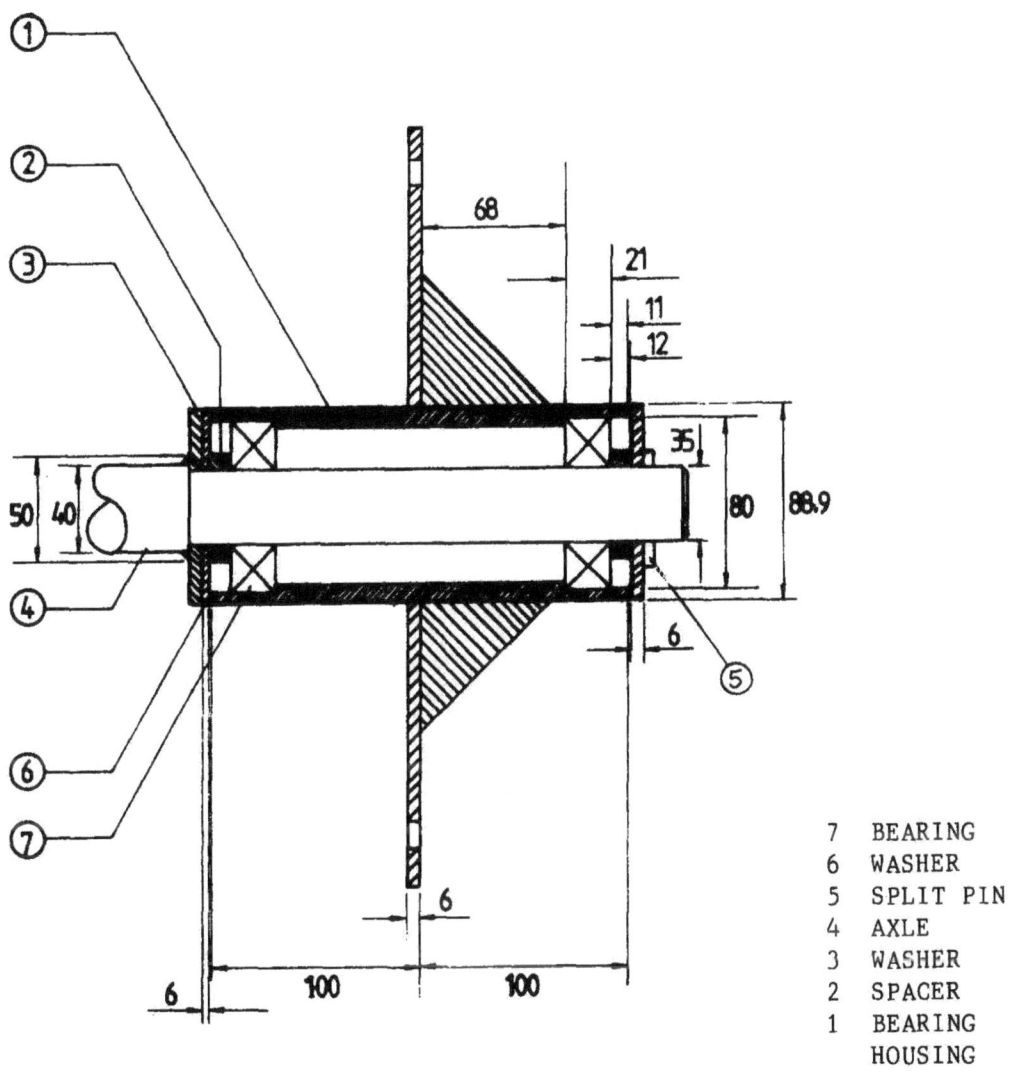

7	BEARING
6	WASHER
5	SPLIT PIN
4	AXLE
3	WASHER
2	SPACER
1	BEARING HOUSING
PART NO.	DESCRIPTION

Figure 3.20 Typical hub-mounted arrangement of ball bearings (to suit wheel shown in Figure 3.18).

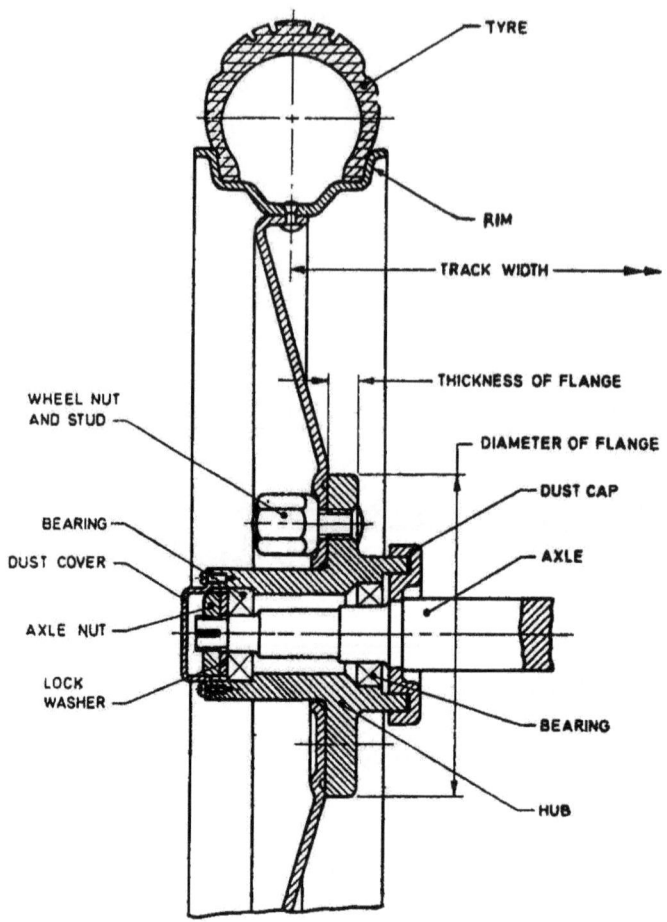

Figure 3.21 Hub and wheel assembly with tapered roller bearings.
Source: Indian Standard 4930-1968 Guide for axle assembly for animal drawn vehicles.

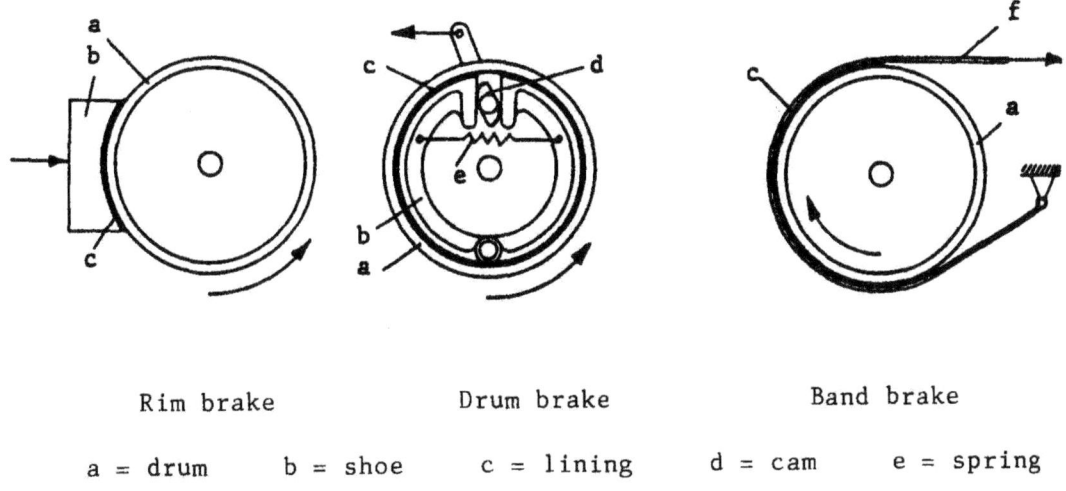

Rim brake   Drum brake   Band brake

a = drum   b = shoe   c = lining   d = cam   e = spring

Figure 3.22   Three types of brake.

Figure 3.23   Wooden block brakes and operating mechanism:
United Republic of Tanzania.

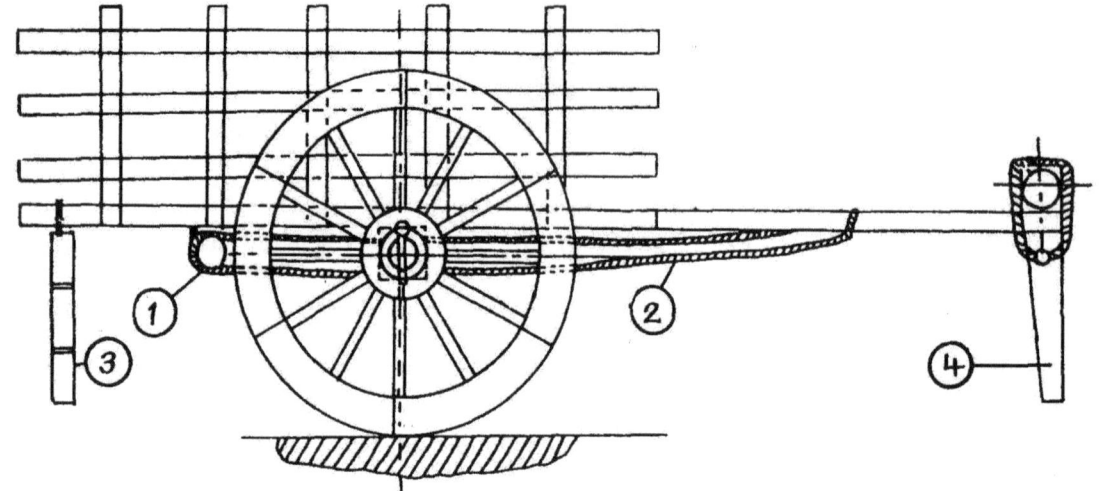

1. Pole brake
2. Rope (to actuate brake)
3. Rear parking support
4. Front parking support

Figure 3.24 Simple braking arrangement (traditional Indian wooden-wheeled cart).
Source: Dunlop India Ltd.

CHAPTER 4: MANUFACTURING ASPECTS

4.1 Introduction

Certain aspects of manufacturing have already been considered in chapter 3, because of their relevance to the design process. This chapter is concerned with the organisation, management and production engineering aspects of manufacture, and considers the advantages, disadvantages and practical implications of manufacturing carts at different scales of production. It also presents various methods of improving production efficiency to increase productivity, reduce costs and achieve good product quality. Finally the chapter analyses the breakdown of manufacturing costs, and discusses the considerations involved in setting sales prices.

4.2 Methods and Scale of Production

There is no clearly defined dividing line between small-, medium- and large-scale production of animal carts, so manufacturers are characterised here by the types of skills and machinery employed, the types of operation which they carry out and the location of the industry. In many cases cart manufacturers will buy in some components, rather than make everything themselves, so different methods and scales of manufacture may be involved in making a complete cart. For example, wheel/axle assemblies with rolling element bearings, pressed steel wheels and pneumatic tyres might be made on a large scale and supplied to individuals and smaller scale enterprises to build the remainder of the cart.

4.2.1 Village Craftworkers

In some Asian countries, traditional skills of cart making are well established at village level, and the methods used have changed little over many years. All parts of the cart can be made in the village, using a considerable degree of skill and little equipment other than hand tools. Most parts of these traditional carts are made of wood, although steel is often used for axles and tyres.

Where craft skills are not specifically related to making carts, more bought-in components, either new or from scrap motor vehicles, will be used. Woodworking and basic metalworking skills are used to make cart frames, bodywork and hitching arrangements. Harnesses, which are made of different materials and require a similar level but different type of skill, will usually be made separately, sometimes by the owner of the animal(s). A village craftworker will manufacture one cart at a time to order only. The cart design may well be adapted to the requirements of a particular customer, who may also supply the materials. Village craftworkers also maintain the local carts, even if they were manufactured elsewhere.

In urban areas, informal sector workshops can make carts in a similar way to village craftworkers. Blacksmithing and a higher level of metalworking skills are likely to be available, as well as some simple machinery such as welding equipment. Consequently steel is likely to be used for a greater proportion of the components.

The details of construction of carts made by craftworkers vary widely according to local requirements and the manufacturers' and customers' preferences. In India traditional cart designs have evolved into distinct regional types. Many of the detail variations in the designs have evolved over a long period of time to suit different local conditions such as route characteristics, typical size of animals and the availability of materials.

<u>Advantages</u> of this level of small-scale informal sector production include:

- low cost - carts made in this way are often the cheapest available;

- responsive to local requirements - the manufacturer is in close contact with users and can therefore learn from their experience and improve the design accordingly. It is also easier to modify designs to suit customer requirements when only one, or at most a few, carts are being made at one time;

- simple distribution (to local customers only);

- little or no capital investment required;

- uses primarily local resources.

<u>Disadvantages</u> of this type of small-scale production include:

- quality of design and construction is variable since it is dependent on individual experience and skill;

- low productivity - lack of engineering resources and machinery prevents the use of labour-saving techniques;

- little innovation by manufacturer - minor modifications and improvements can be made readily, but significant innovations or the development of new designs will occur only slowly;

- because of the dispersed and unco-ordinated nature of this type of production it is difficult for outside assistance to be applied effectively to introduce innovation and raise skill levels;

- few promotional skills or resources available to expand production and encourage use of carts;

- supply of raw materials and components variable in quality, availability and price - manufacturers who place small orders with wholesalers tend to receive the worst material when good quality supplies are limited, and they have little control over the price charged.

4.2.2 Formal Sector De-Centralised Workshops

Formal sector workshops are characterised by the use of electrically-powered equipment for cutting, turning, bending and welding steel, and by the use primarily of new, rather than scrap, materials. The category includes a wide range of organisations, including private companies, state-owned enterprises, church or charity-funded centres, and government-sponsored development schemes. Production will typically be on a small or medium scale and the industry may be located in a rural or an urban area. A workshop of this level will normally only be able to cater to the market for carts in its own region of the country. It is likely that carts will be only one of a range of related products, such as agricultural equipment, made by the workshop, which may also undertake general engineering fabrication work. The workshop may produce a range of related designs of carts, and there may be considerable variation between different manufacturers' products.

The availability of engineering resources and machinery gives these formal sector workshops the capability to produce a wide range of components including: bodywork and frame (including special purpose bodies); steel wheels (solid and split rim), steel axles for two- and four-wheeled carts, rubber and steel tyres; plain bearings, leaf springs; wheel/axle assemblies; rim and axle brakes; harnesses and hitching equipment. However a particular workshop may decide that it is cheaper, or more efficient, to buy in certain of these components. Items such as rolling element bearings or drum brake assemblies may be bought in from specialist suppliers. Steel will need to be used to a much larger extent than wood, except possibly for bodywork.

<u>Advantages</u> of this level of production include:

- resources and expertise available to achieve good quality construction and often to develop, adapt and improve designs;

- use of machinery and special tooling enables increased productivity of labour - this can result in a lower price to the customer if labour is a significant proportion of the production cost;

- responsive to local requirements - geographic decentralisation enables the manufacturer to adapt designs to suit regional conditions. Feedback from users is likely to be limited however to that from nearby users unless the workshop has a well developed marketing network;

- formal organisation facilitates use of outside expertise and assistance;

- resources available to promote use and sales of carts;

- some control over raw material supplies and prices.

Disadvantages of this type of production include:

- possible distribution difficulties and high cost of transport to customer (dependent on production volume relative to geographic extent and size of local demand);

- repair service limited to nearby users unless marketing network is well developed;

- machinery and materials often imported and may be difficult and/or expensive to obtain — which may result in a high price to the customer, and problems in maintenance of equipment.

4.2.3 Centralised Large-Scale Production

Agricultural equipment can be manufactured by large organisations to supply a national market. Animal-drawn carts might be included in a wide range of such products. This type of industry has the potential to achieve high quality production at low unit cost by using high capacity machinery. However, achieving this potential is highly dependent on the efficient organisation and management of human, capital, financial and material resources, and in practice there are wide variations in the quality of output achieved.

Components which can be made by large-scale industries include: bodywork and frame; steel wheels; pneumatic and solid tyres; plain and rolling element bearings; leaf springs; all types of brake; axles for two- and four-wheeled carts; wheel/axle assemblies; and hitching equipment.

Large-scale production is the only way of making some of these components, such as rolling element bearings and pneumatic tyres, at a reasonable cost and quality. For some others, such as wheels for pneumatic tyres, steel axles and hub brakes, efficient large-scale production should offer technical and cost advantages. In China, India and Vietnam, the large-scale production of critical components (wheels, axles, bearings) which are supplied to small-scale cart manufacturers, has stimulated the production and use of carts. The easy availability of such components has provided the mechanism to improve the specification and performance of traditional carts by small-scale manufacturers. In China and Vietnam these large industries have been established and supported by government policy to encourage the use of animal-drawn carts. In India they have developed through private initiative.

Advantages of large-scale production include:

- economies of scale and high productivity of labour possible (but not always achieved);

- resources and expertise available to develop, adapt and improve designs and achieve good quality construction;

- resources available, including possible government backing, to promote use and sales of carts;

- control of local raw material supplies possible - also better access to imported supplies than smaller scale industries.

<u>Disadvantages</u> of large scale production include:

- not responsive to local needs - where complete carts are made, particular local requirements are unlikely to be met unless a range of different carts is made. Difficult to make variations to standard designs to suit customer requirements;

- difficult to obtain feedback from users - may inhibit improvement and innovation;

- marketing/distribution organisation required;

- high cost of transport to customer (for complete carts);

- no repair service (unless provided as part of marketing/distribution organisation);

- large capital investment required, often for imported equipment and expertise;

- production efficiency and construction quality highly dependent on organisation and management.

4.3 Production Engineering

The overall aim of any cart manufacturer will be to sell products over a long period of time at a price which will make a profit. This is best achieved by maximising the quality and effectiveness of the product within the constraints imposed by the price at which the carts are sold. The design of the product is clearly a key issue in achieving this balance. However there is also considerable scope for achieving good construction quality and high productivity by the application of efficient production engineering methods.

4.3.1 Production Tooling

Production tooling requires capital investment, although in many cases this may consist largely of the time necessary to design and construct it together with a limited allowance for materials. This investment cost must be recovered from the sale of carts, so the size of the investment, and hence the amount and complexity of the tooling, will be limited by the production volume over which its cost can be spread.

Small-scale craftworkers at village level are unlikely to use any specialised production tooling other than templates for marking out and checking dimensions. Their products are made one at a time and the design is frequently altered to suit customer requirements and to make use of different raw, often scrap, materials. The craftworker relies largely on skill and experience rather than tooling to achieve satisfactory strength and quality of construction.

At higher production rates a wide range of tooling may be used. These include, in approximate order of cost and complexity:

1. <u>Templates</u>: for marking out by hand the shapes and lengths of materials and the position of holes prior to cutting and drilling - used, for example, in making bodywork and frame components.

2. <u>Drilling Jigs</u>: for accurately positioning holes which need to be aligned with others for subsequent assembly or in use - used, for example, to ensure accurate location of axle on frame and of components on axle.

3. <u>Welding Fixtures</u>: for accurate positioning, alignment and clamping of components to be joined by welding - used, for example, in the construction of frames, axles and wheels.

4. <u>Modifications to General-purpose Machines</u>: for rapid production of turned and other machined components. Modifications range from specially shaped cutting tools through to semi-permanent fixtures on the machine - used, for example, in making bearings, hubs and brake components.

5. <u>Small General-purpose Press Tools</u>: for rapid bending and punching of thin materials on hand-operated machines - used, for example, to make bodywork, brake components, special washers and small brackets.

6. <u>Special-purpose Machines</u>: for rapid, high-volume production of turned and other machined components and for metal forming - used, for example, to make rolling element bearings and pressed steel wheels.

In designing production tooling for the manufacture of animal-drawn carts, it is important to ensure that:

- it is simple to use;
- it is simple to make and repair;
- materials can <u>only</u> be located in the correct position;
- dimensional variations of raw materials are allowed for;
- critical points are accurately located.

Accuracy in the construction of production tooling is vital since any error will be repeated on every component produced from the tooling. Robustness and resistance to wear are also essential for long term use.

It is a prerequisite for, and indeed the objective of the use of production tooling, that every component made with it is identical. This helps to achieve good product quality by ensuring that a satisfactory design is repeated consistently. Good productivity is achieved by reducing the time required for manufacturing operations, and by reducing wastage and avoiding the need for time-consuming 'fitting' operations during assembly. It should also ensure that spares and replacements parts can be fitted without problems to carts produced from the tooling.

A further benefit of production tooling is that it enables a skilled operator to produce to a higher standard, and enables many jobs to be carried out by less skilled people than would otherwise be necessary. In general, the more elaborate and costly the tooling, the less skill is required to use it. This effect of the use of production tooling is often referred to as 'de-skilling', but it is more accurately described as 'skill enhancement'. For example, in welded assemblies the strength and appearance of the weld itself is significantly affected by the size of gap between the materials being joined, and the dimensional accuracy of the assembly is affected by distortion caused by the welding process. By using a welding fixture, the materials can be accurately positioned, which controls the gap size, and clamped to prevent distortion. Considerable skill and time is needed to achieve the same weld quality and accuracy by hand.

One drawback of using production tooling is that variations to the standard design to meet individual customer requirements are more difficult to make, because the equipment is designed to produce identical components.

4.3.2 Quality Control Procedures

Quality control procedures are important to ensure overall product quality and to minimise the number of rejected components and the time wasted in correcting faults. In many cases, dimensional checks by measurement and visual inspections are all that is required. The production tooling itself can often be designed to provide quality control checks automatically, e.g. by preventing faulty components from fitting into jigs and fixtures, or by dimensions being compared with a template. Special gauges may be used to check that critical dimensions of components such as bearings, which must fit closely onto axles and into hubs, are within specified tolerances. The production workers themselves should carry out the quality control checks as far as possible so that errors may be corrected quickly before repetition, and to encourage individual responsibility for quality standards. However it is usually desirable for supervisory staff to complement these with sample checks.

It is also useful to carry out quality control checks of components and materials which are bought in. There can be substantial differences between specified and actual sizes of raw materials, and if a particular item is not available, suppliers may send the nearest equivalent without informing the manufacturer. If checks are made and errors rectified before the material is needed for production, a good deal of time may be saved. It will also be easier to return goods to the supplier if errors are notified soon after they are received.

4.4 Production Organisation and Management

The overall efficiency and cost of production is affected not just by the engineering of the production process, but also by its organisation and management. In particular:

- in medium- or large-scale production, variations to the standard design will involve extra work and expense. The need to charge the customer the full additional cost of this should be balanced against the desirability of offering a range of options to suit particular requirements;

- in batch production, groups of components which are made from the same material or require similar types of machining, can be made at the same time, to reduce machine set-up times;

- the allocation of tasks can be planned in advance to spread them evenly between the workforce to reduce idle time;

- ordering procedures should aim to minimise material stocks and the capital tied up in them. This is easy when suppliers can be relied upon to deliver quickly. Where supplies are less reliable, the savings from maintaining low stock levels must be balanced against the possible delays in production caused by running out of materials at the right time;

- in batch production, more efficient use is made of storage and working space, and capital, by making small batches often rather than large batches infrequently. This must be balanced against the time lost in setting up machines and tooling for different operations and the administrative costs of frequent ordering.

4.4.1 Production Costs

In order to set up and operate a successful cart manufacturing industry it is important to be able to make accurate estimates of the costs of producing carts. Because of the wide variation in production methods and types of cart which can be made, in addition to wide variations in costs in different countries, there is little to be gained by quoting indicative costs for one particular set of circumstances. The information given below is intended to provide the basis for:

a) preparing estimates of production costs for a proposed cart manufacturing enterprise and for analysing how the unit production cost will vary with output. These estimates are essential in assessing the viability of an enterprise, and in determining the level of output that must be achieved to provide an acceptable return on the investment.

b) calculating accurately the unit cost of production in an enterprise that is already manufacturing carts, possibly in addition to other products. It is often the case that enterprises are not fully aware of their own costs. However such information is essential to the efficient management of the enterprise:

   i) to ensure that selling prices are set so that each product brings an income to the enterprise that reflects its costs;

   ii) to identify opportunities for reducing the cost of manufacturing the product.

There are three elements that make up the total cost of producing carts:

- direct labour cost;
- direct material cost;
- overheads.

Each of these elements is discussed below, followed by consideration of how they are combined to calculate the total unit production cost of a cart.

Direct labour cost

This is the cost of the labour time actually involved in making the carts, that is in machining and fabricating components, in assembling them and in finishing operations such as painting, etc.

For an industry making only one type of cart, the direct labour cost per cart is most easily calculated as:

$$\frac{L \times W}{C}$$

where

L = number of direct labour persons employed
W = wage cost per person per period of time (week, month or year)
C = number of carts produced per period of time (week, month or year)

Note that the wage cost per person must include the wage actually paid to the employee, plus any directly associated costs incurred by the employer (e.g. employee insurance, labour tax).

If the industry produces a range of carts with different labour inputs, or a range of products including carts, then the direct labour cost per cart is most easily calculated as:

(no. of hours labour involved in manufacturing the cart) x (hourly wage rate)

The wage rate must again include directly associated costs incurred by the employer.

It is often the case that different grades of labour, with different wage levels, are employed in manufacturing carts. The cost per cart must then be calculated separately for each grade of labour, and these elements added together to give the unit direct labour cost. For an existing enterprise data on the labour input per cart will be available from written records or from experience. When planning a new enterprise the labour cost must be calculated from an estimate of the labour input required.

The above analysis shows that it is relatively straightforward to calculate unit direct labour cost. It also emphasises the importance of utilising labour efficiently. If there is insufficient work to keep the labour force busy, then the cost per cart will increase. However any measure to increase labour productivity by reducing the number of hours input per cart will reduce the unit labour cost. (Note that such measures may involve investment in equipment or in more expensive materials. This cost must be set against the saving in labour cost to decide whether the investment is worthwhile).

Direct materials cost

This is the cost to the manufacturer of the raw materials (steel, wood, paint, etc.) purchased for further processing, and the bought-in components such as bearings and pneumatic tyres. The calculation of direct materials cost per cart is fairly straightforward, based either on records of purchases for an existing industry, or suppliers' quotations for a new enterprise. However some allowance must be made for wastage since:

- when cutting components from standard lengths or sheets of material, there will always be pieces left over which are the wrong size to make anything useful;

- even the most reliable workers occasionally make mistakes, resulting in some material or component being scrapped.

Where imported items are purchased directly from overseas by the cart manufacturer, the cost must include transportation and handling charges, customs duties, and the cost of obtaining the foreign exchange. Where such items are purchased locally from an importer, these costs will be built into the importer's price.

Savings in direct materials costs can be achieved by:

- organising production, and specifying the size of components, to minimise material wastage;

- identifying a cheaper source of supply than the existing supplier (though it is important to ensure that the materials or components from the new source of supply are of suitable quality, strength and reliability);

- negotiating discounts for repeat or larger orders (in the latter case the saving on unit cost from purchasing larger quantities must be set against the additional cost of carrying larger stocks).

Overheads

The overheads comprise all the other costs which are involved in operating the business but which, unlike direct labour and direct materials, cannot be directly attributed to the manufacture of an individual product. They include all the day-to-day costs of running the business, together with the investment costs. Each of the elements which go to make up the total overhead cost are discussed below.

<u>Working capital</u> Any manufacturing business will have money tied up in the value of the materials and components which have been purchased but not yet processed, and the products which have been manufactured but not yet sold and paid for. The value of these items (finished products held in stock should be valued at total production cost) represents the working capital tied up in the business. If this working capital must be borrowed then the interest payable is a cost to the enterprise.[1]

<u>Plant and equipment</u> Money must be invested to purchase all the machinery and equipment used in manufacturing the carts, including tooling, jigs and fixtures, together with the office furniture and equipment (e.g. typewriters) necessary to administer the business. The depreciation of this investment is a cost to the business. Appropriate depreciation rates are a matter to be decided by local circumstances based on a realistic estimate of the useful life of the items. For example, it is common to depreciate office equipment at 25% per annum and manufacturing plant at 15%. In practice most items of plant and equipment will always have some residual value (e.g. a machine which is worn out and no longer operable will still have some value as scrap metal). This can be reflected by calculating depreciation on the <u>remaining value</u> of the equipment. For example if a depreciation rate of 25% is selected, in the first year the cost would be 25% of the purchase value of the equipment. In the second year it would be 25% of 75% of the purchase value, etc.

If the enterprise has borrowed money to purchase the equipment, then the interest payable is a cost to the business.[1] A company may decide to rent or to lease some items of equipment, rather than investing in

---

1. If the capital is provided from the company's cash reserve, then the interest that could have been earned by investing this money elsewhere should be considered as a cost to the company (i.e. the opportunity cost for the capital). However in practice it may be more convenient to use this figure as a basis for determining the minimum level of profitability that is necessary to make the investment in the company worthwhile.

their purchase. In this case the cost to the enterprise is the rental or leasing payments.

Buildings and land If the manufacturing company purchases the buildings and land where it operates, then the interest payable on any money borrowed for the purpose,[1] plus the depreciation of the facilities, is a cost to the business. In practice a depreciation rate of zero is normally used for land since in many cases its real value will increase with time. A low depreciation rate of between 2% and 4% is normally assumed for buildings. If the company rents the buildings it uses then their cost is represented by the rental payments.

Indirect labour All but the smallest manufacturing businesses will employ persons other than those directly involved in producing the products. The indirect labour might include, for example, cleaners, secretaries, supervisory staff, management and marketing staff. Their wages, and any associated costs, make up the indirect labour cost.

Indirect materials Any manufacturing business will purchase certain materials which do not constitute part of the products it produces. For example, indirect production materials (sometimes called consumables) will include lubricants for machinery, gas for welding and welding rods, cleaning materials etc. In addition there are the costs of the consumable administrative materials, such as stationery.

Utilities These are the services purchased by the company including power supplies (electricity, gas, etc.) and water supply.

Maintenance Any company will incur costs in the maintenance of its plant and buildings. These are normally estimated as follows:

>   plant   – 5% of purchase value per annum;
>   buildings – 2% of purchase value per annum.

Insurance Depending on local legal requirements, or on its own judgement of what is prudent, a company may have to insure against theft, damage caused by fire, injuries to employees, etc.

Taxes Depending on local regulations a company is likely to have to pay taxes in one form or another, e.g. rates, property tax and land tax. Note that sales tax is not a part of production cost. Nor is a tax on profits, though both of these may influence the selling price set for the product.

---

1. If the capital is provided from the company's cash reserve, then the interest that could have been earned by investing this money elsewhere should be considered as a cost to the company (i.e. the opportunity cost for the capital). However in practice it may be more convenient to use this figure as a basis for determining the minimum level of profitability that is necessary to make the investment in the company worthwhile.

Advertising costs Many of the costs associated with selling the carts produced by the company have already been covered under other overhead categories, i.e. sales staff (indirect labour), brochures (stationery) etc. However any advertisements placed in newspapers, magazines, etc., represent a cost to the company.

For an existing business the various overhead costs can be calculated from written records and from experience. When planning a new enterprise estimates can be obtained by investigating current market values (e.g. for buildings), by obtaining quotations from suppliers, and by preparing budget projections for the various overhead items.

For management purposes it is sometimes useful, particularly in a larger enterprise, to separate overhead costs into categories. For example, to understand how money is being spent and to identify opportunities for savings, it may be useful to divide overheads into those related to the manufacture of the products (e.g. the depreciation of machinery), those related to administration and management, and those related to marketing.

It is worth noting that the overhead costs described above do not include the cost of delivering or transporting the goods to the customer. This is because it is normal practice to calculate the total cost of the product ex-factory (i.e. the cost when it leaves the factory) and to add delivery costs as an additional charge to the customer. Because animal carts are large and heavy relative to their value, the cost of transport for delivery can be high, especially if long distances are involved. This can be a factor in determining the geographic size of the market that can be served from a particular factory, and in deciding whether it is worthwhile to supply the cart in unassembled form, or as a wheel/axle/frame assembly to which the customer can fit his own bodywork.

Calculation of total unit production cost

The above sections have described how to calculate or estimate the direct labour and material costs per product, and the overhead costs of operating the business. It is usually most convenient to calculate the overhead costs on an annual basis, i.e. to determine the total overhead cost per annum of the business. The problem that then remains is to distribute the overhead cost between all the products produced per annum in order to determine the total unit production cost of each product. Thus production cost per product is expressed as:

direct labour cost per product + direct material cost per product + overhead cost per product.

For the very simplest type of cart manufacturing enterprise, that is a village carpenter working alone making carts from local materials, this calculation is very straightforward. His overhead costs will be minimal (his equipment will normally consist only of hand tools and templates, and his premises will probably be a simple structure to provide protection from the weather) and his labour cost will simply be for his own time. Thus his selling price for a cart can be calculated by adding to the material cost the amount he expects and wishes to earn for the time he has devoted to building the cart.

For any enterprise larger than this one-man, low-overhead example, it is necessary first to determine total unit production cost, and then determine selling price (selling price is discussed in the next section). For an enterprise whose only product is one model of cart, the calculation of total unit product cost is straightforward. The total overhead cost per annum of the enterprise is divided by the number of carts produced to give the overhead cost per cart. This is added to the labour and material costs to give the unit production cost.

If the enterprise produces a range of different carts with different labour and material inputs, or manufactures a variety of products including carts, then the problem is to find an equitable means of distributing the overheads amongst the various products. The aim is to use a method which ensures that each product carries its fair share of overheads, but which is no more complicated than necessary. One method which is commonly used is to calculate what total overhead costs/annum are as a percentage of total labour cost/annum. The overheads cost for an individual product is then calculated as that percentage of the direct labour cost of the product. This system works well as long as the range of products manufactured all make a similar call on overheads. However if one product makes a heavier call on overheads than others (e.g. by using expensive, specialised manufacturing equipment, or by having high marketing costs), then the analysis must be more complicated and disaggregate different categories of overhead.

An alternative method is used by many small-scale engineering industries in India. The unit labour and overhead costs are calculated in a single amount as a percentage of the raw materials (steel and timber) cost of the product. The percentage used is based on experience of the overall costs of the enterprise. Bought-in components are costed as a separate item, so that the total unit production cost is:

materials cost + labour and overheads (as a percentage of materials) + bought-in components cost.

This method is not very accurate as it does not reflect the complexity of the manufacturing processes involved, nor does it encourage measures to reduce labour costs. However with experience it can work reasonably well where the cost of labour is low relative to material costs, as is typical in many developing countries.

4.4.2 Selling Price

The selling price of the cart will be of over-riding importance in determining whether it will be purchased by customers. Thus pricing is important in determining the size of the market, and the type of cart for which there is the greatest demand. For example, for a small farmer, a cart will represent a substantial investment, especially if credit is not available, and in this case the quality, specification and efficiency of the cart will be of a secondary importance to price.

The key to a successful cart manufacturing enterprise is to produce and sell carts of a specification and at a price which generates a satisfactory level of demand, while providing an acceptable profit margin over the production cost. Different types of enterprise will have different definitions of 'acceptable profit margin'. A commercial company will normally be able to define the minimum level of profit that is acceptable, taking account of interest foregone on money invested in the business, and of any tax that will be due on profits. This minimum acceptable profit will be based on either the desired return on the investment or on a minimum level of income that is required. However carts may also be produced by organisations which have developmental rather than commercial objectives and which are prepared to sell carts at cost (i.e. with zero profit) or to subsidise the sales price. It is desirable that such an organisation should operate on a commercial basis in the sense of knowing its production costs accurately, and then setting the selling price according to its developmental objectives. For example, an organisation that decides to sell 'at cost' should decide whether it wishes to recover all costs, or only operating costs (excluding investment overheads, or only direct costs, excluding all overheads). Similarly organisations wishing to subsidise sales should examine the total production costs and then decide the level of subsidy to offer.

In simple terms, the selling price of a cart is calculated by adding the desired profit margin to the production cost, and then adding any taxation and distribution or delivery charges that have to be recovered. (Note that for developmental organisations the profit margin may be zero or negative). However there are other factors which may influence the selling price that is set:

a) in some countries it may be necessary to include an allowance in the standard selling price for bargaining with the customer;

b) if the manufacturer sells through agents or retailers, rather than direct to customers, then his pricing policy must not only provide him with an adequate profit while offering the cart to the customer at an acceptable price, but also allow the agent to make a reasonable return. When marketing through an agent the manufacturer may offer an incentive to increase sales, for example by giving a reduction in unit price to the agent for increased quantities sold;

c) in some countries there are government schemes to support the purchase of agricultural equipment by farmers, particularly in the small-scale sector. It may well be worthwhile for a cart manufacturer to price his products so as to ensure their inclusion in the scheme;

d) if a manufacturer adds carts to an existing range of products, and thereby uses his resources more efficiently, he may be able to sell the carts at a lower profit margin because some of the overhead costs are already being fully recovered from the other products.

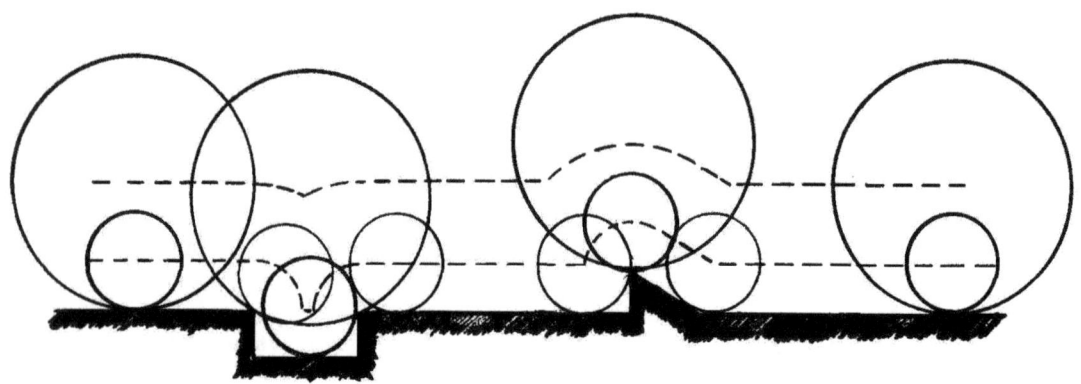

---- Path of wheel centres

Figure A1. Effect of wheel diameter on rolling resistance. Source: Reference 17.

ANNEX: TRACTIVE EFFORT

Despite the apparent simplicity of an animal-drawn cart, there are many forces which act upon it, and there are many variables which affect its performance. An engineering analysis of two-wheeled bullock carts has been carried out by Raghavan and Nagendra (20), which considers these forces and variables in detail. As far as the owner or user is concerned it is the tractive effort required to pull the cart which is crucial, since this determines the useful payload. This is the maximum load that can be carried, and will vary according to the difference between the tractive effort required to pull the unloaded cart and the tractive effort available from the animal(s), up to a limit imposed by the strength of the cart.

The tractive effort required is determined by many factors:

- gradient of the terrain;
- roughness of the route surface;
- hardness of the route surface;
- total weight of the cart (weight of cart itself plus payload);
- position of the centre of gravity of the total weight;
- diameter of the wheels;
- width of the wheel rim;
- type of tyre;
- bearing friction;
- line of draught;
- acceleration of the cart.

A considerable amount of research has been carried out to investigate the tractive effort requirement of different types of two-wheeled carts under a variety of operating conditions. Unfortunately, few of the results are directly comparable because there are so many variations of the parameters defined above. The following observations on the effect of the different parameters are based on these research reports:

RAGHAVAN, M.R. and H.R. NAGENDRA. Engineering analysis of the two wheel bullock cart design. (20)

RAGHAVAN, M.R. and D.L. PRASANNA RAO. Experimental study of forces in a bullock cart. (6)

DHIR, M.P. and S.R. BINDRA. The relative tractive efficiency of steel-tyred and pneumatic-tyred bullock carts on earthen tracks. (7)

SAYER, W. Tests on Dunlop pneumatic equipment for farm carts. (8)

ANON. Improvement of the existing design of bullock carts in Bangladesh. (9)

Gradient of the terrain

The theoretical analysis of Raghavan and Nagendra demonstrates that the tractive effort is affected significantly by the terrain gradient. In general, pull parallel to ground will increase by approximately 10kgf per tonne total weight for each one per cent increase in gradient. For a typical cart with a balanced load, the pull required is zero on a down slope of 11 per cent. If the down gradient is greater than this the cart must be braked, either by the animal(s) or with a mechanical brake. The diameter of the wheel has little effect on the effort required on different gradients.

Roughness and hardness of the route surface

The effect of surface roughness and hardness on the rolling resistance of carts, and hence the tractive effort required, is very complex. None of the researchers attempted to quantify these factors, but all of them conducted tests on different types of surface. Raghavan and Prasanna noted that the dynamic frictional resistance of a dry, hard mud road was some 30% greater than a tarmac road for a steel-rimmed wooden-wheeled cart, but about the same for a pneumatic-tyred cart. For both carts the resistance of grassy terrain was about 100% greater than a tarmac road. Dhir and Bindra found that, on a concrete track, resistance was similar for all types of cart, but recorded considerable variations on other surfaces. In general, the tractive effort required on dry sand was about 10 times that on concrete, reducing to about 5 times as much when the sand was wet or rutted; dry soil required about 2-3 times as much effort with pneumatic tyres or 6-8 times with wooden or steel wheels; in wet soil 15cm deep all wheels were similar at 6-8 times the value for concrete, but in 30cm wet soil pneumatic tyres require about 15 times the effort on concrete compared to 10-12 times for wood and steel wheels, with little change in the values when the surface was rutted. Sayer recorded that wooden-wheeled carts required 3-4 times the effort needed with pneumatic tyres on ploughed land, but only slightly more effort was needed on an earth road.

Total weight of the cart

The theoretical work of Raghavan and Nagendra states that variations in the laden weight of the cart on any terrain have only an insignificant effect on the horizontal pull required, but this is not borne out in practice. Dhir and Bindra's experiments were conducted on a variety of terrains with gross loads of 750 and 1,000kg, and the results indicate that the tractive effort for the lighter load was generally about 15% less than for the heavier load. The work in Bangladesh with wooden-wheeled carts with both roller and cast iron bush bearings indicate little change in tractive effort with changes in load for gross loads above 1,500kg on paved roads, but on earth roads and with lighter loads on paved roads the relationship is approximately linear, and the magnitude of the change is significant.

Position of the centre of gravity of the total weight

Raghavan and Nagendra state that the position of the centre of gravity of the load has an insignificant effect on the horizontal pull required, but that it has a profound influence on the vertical loading on the animal(s). On flat ground, it is the horizontal position of the centre of gravity which is most important, but the vertical position above the axle is also important on gradients. The inertia of the total load will also affect the vertical loading on the animals when braking and accelerating, its importance also being determined by the vertical position of the centre of gravity. In order to minimise these variations in vertical loading the centre of gravity should be close to the cart axle.

Diameter of the wheels

Wheel diameter has an important effect on the tractive effort required. On rough roads, larger diameter wheels will cause the wheels, and hence the cart, to change direction less when traversing bumps and potholes, as shown in Figure A1, which reduces the magnitude of the pull required. The effect of bearing friction is also less with a larger diameter wheel. Raghavan and Prasanna show that wheel diameter has a dramatic effect on the vertical load on the animal(s). With a high coefficient of rolling friction on level ground, the vertical load is 550% greater for a cart with 0.61m wheels than with 1.83m wheels. A larger wheel does increase the weight of the cart however. Vagh presented data on the tractive effort of wooden wheels of different diameters, which varied approximately linearly between 32kgf per tonne total cart weight for a 1.6m diameter wheel and 65kgf per tonne for a 0.75m diameter wheel.

Width of the wheel rim

Vagh also stated that, for solid wheels, wider rims reduce tractive effort, quoting figures which indicate a reduction of about 15-20% by increasing the rim width from 50mm to 87mm.

Type of tyre

Raghavan and Prasanna's tests show that the dynamic effective coefficient of friction for a cart with steel-rimmed wooden wheels is about 30% lower than a pneumatic-tyred cart on tarmac and grassy terrain, whereas on a mud road the coefficient for steel-rimmed wheels is slightly higher than with pneumatic tyres. Evidence from the other references clearly demonstrates that the most efficient type of tyre for a cart depends on the route surface, solid wheels tending to be slightly better on hard surfaces, pneumatic tyres slightly better on soft ground. Some surprising results are worth noting however. Dhir and Bindra found that on rutted dry sand and dry soil pneumatic tyres are markedly better, whilst in deep wet soil they are considerably worse. Vagh recorded that on ploughed land a pneumatic-tyred cart required less than a quarter of the effort of a traditional wooden wheeled cart. Raghavan and Prasanna make the point that solid wheels cause large variations in the vertical load on the animal(s), which presumably causes considerable discomfort and reduces their work output. Pneumatic tyres are considerably better in this respect, because of their shock absorbing properties.

Bearing friction

Raghavan and Prasanna demonstrate that the contribution of bearing friction to the effective coefficient of rolling friction is small, and quote figures of 3% and 8% respectively for wheel diameters of 1.83m and 0.61m. However the precise contribution will of course vary according to the relative efficiencies of the bearing and the wheel. Experiments in Bangladesh indicate that cast iron bush bearings have a similar coefficient of friction to tapered roller bearings with gross loads of about 1,500kg or less, but the latter are slightly better with bigger loads.

Line of draught

The line of draught of a cart passes through the wheel axle and the point at which the animal applies its force to the harness. The draught force can be considered as having a horizontal component which provides the useful pulling force, and a vertical component which is wasted. The closer the line of draught is to the horizontal the smaller will be the vertical component caused by rolling friction when the cart is in motion. A horizontal line of draught can be achieved by matching the diameter of the wheels to the height of the animal though in practice this can have other disadvantages. Other vertical forces will also act on the animal caused by unbalanced loads on the cart and the inertia of the load, so the resultant draught force will not usually act in the direction of the line of draught.

Acceleration of cart

Raghavan and Nagendra demonstrate that, although the forces caused by the inertia of the load when accelerating and braking are small in slow-moving vehicles like animal carts, they can cause significant variations in the vertical load on the animal(s), especially when the centre of gravity of the load is far from the wheel axle. This appears to be particularly important in the case of bullock carts which, at their normal operating speed of 3-4km per hour, are pulled in a rather discontinuous manner. More significant is that the pull required to start a cart moving is substantially greater than that required to keep it in motion. Raghavan and Prasanna measured the static coefficient of friction for steel-rimmed wooden wheeled carts to be between 1.5 and 6 times higher than the dynamic coefficient of friction. Since most animals can exert an instantaneous pull several times their normal average pull, this is not a great problem unless frequent starting and stopping is necessary.

REFERENCES

1. BIRD, A. Roads and vehicles. London, Arrow Books, 1973.

2. GERAINT JENKINS, J. The English farm waggon: origins and structure. Newton Abbot, David and Charles, 1972.

3. RAMASWAMY, N.S., The management of animal energy resources and the modernisation of the bullock cart system. Bangalore, Indian Institute of Management, 1979.

4. PLUMBE, A.J. and D.J. SAVAGE, Bullock cart haulage in Sri Lanka. Department of the Environment Department of Transport TRRL Laboratory Report LR1006. Crowthorne, Transport and Road Research Laboratory, 1981.

5. BUREAU OF HIGHWAYS OF MINISTRY OF COMMUNICATIONS PEOPLE'S REPUBLIC OF CHINA. China non-motorised vehicle. Economic and Social Commission for Asia and the Pacific. Workshop-cum-Exhibition on the Improvement of Non-motorised Transport. Bangkok, 8-14 March 1983.

6. RAGHAVAN, M.R. and D.L. PRASANNA RAO. 'Experimental study of forces in a bullock cart', in Proc. Indian Acad. Sci., Vol.C2 Part 4, December 1979. pp.435-449

7. DHIR, M.P. and S.R. BINDRA. The relative tractive efficiency of steel-tyred and pneumatic-tyred bullock carts on earthen tracks. Road Research Papers No. 66. Okhla, Delhi, Central Road Research Institute, 1965.

8. SAYER, W. 'Tests on Dunlop pneumatic equipment for farm carts'. Imperial Agriculturalist 1933-34. (Tests conducted at Imperial Institute of Agricultural Research, Pusa).

9. ANON. Improvement of the existing design of bullock carts in Bangladesh. Department of Farm Power and Machinery, Bangladesh Agricultural University, Mymensigh, Bangladesh 1983.

10. ARNOLD, J., The farm waggons of England and Wales. London, John Baker, 1969.

11. GOE, M.R. and R.E. McDOWELL, 'Animal traction: guidelines for utilisation'. Cornell International Agriculture Mimeo. Department of Animal Science. Ithaca, New York. December 1980. (Cornell University).

12. WATSON, P.R. 'Animal traction'. Information Collection and Exchange, Appropriate Technologies for Development Manual Number M-12. Washington, DC, Peace Corps, August 1981.

13. GOWEN, H.C., 'Non-motorised transport in developing countries'. Thesis submitted in partial submission for the degree of Master of Science, Centre for Transport Studies. Cranfield Institute of Technology, September 1984.

14. MUNZINGER, P., Animal traction in Africa. Eschborn, Deutsche Gesellschaft für Technische Zusammenarbeit (GTZ) GmbH, 1982.

15. BARWELL, I. and M. AYRE. The harnessing of draught animals. London, I.T. Publications, 1982.

16. VAGH, B.V., 'A design for bullock cart wheels – Part V: Conclusions' J. Indian Rd. Congr. 15 (2) November 1950.

17. BJORLYKKE and LUNDE. The craft of the wheelwright. Windsor, Profile Books, 1983.

18. ETRTO. Brussels, The European Tyre and Rim Technical Organisation, 1981.

19. COLLETT, J., Oil soaked wood bearings: how to make them and how they perform. London, I.T. Publications, n.d.

20. RAGHAVAN, M.R. and H.R. NAGENDRA. 'Engineering analysis of the two wheeled bullock cart design'. Proc. Indian Acad. Sci., Vol. C2, Part 4, December 1979.

www.ingramcontent.com/pod-product-compliance
Ingram Content Group UK Ltd.
Pitfield, Milton Keynes, MK11 3LW, UK
UKHW050523150426
5217IPUK00026B/1763